SAINT PAUL AND CHRISTIAN CHARITY

BY

STEPHEN HASKELL

Published by New Generation Publishing in 2020

First Edition

ISBN

	Paperback	978-1-80031-570-9
	Ebook	978-1-80031-569-3

www.newgeneration-publishing.com

 New Generation Publishing

FOR PAUL AND JANET

Contents

INTRODUCTION

What need is there to say more when St Paul has said it all and said it so beautifully?

If I speak in the tongues of men and of angels, but have not charity, I am a noisy gong, or a clanging cymbal.

And if I have prophetic powers and understand all mysteries, and all knowledge; and if I have all faith, so as to remove mountains, but have not charity, I am nothing.

If I give away all I have, and if I deliver my body to be burned, but have not charity, I gain nothing.

Charity is patient and kind; charity is not jealous or boastful; it is not arrogant or rude.

Charity does not insist on its own way; it is not irritable or resentful; it does not rejoice at wrong, but rejoices in the right.

Charity bears all things, believes all things, hopes all things, endures all things.

Charity never ends; as for prophecies, they will pass away; as for tongues, they will cease; as for knowledge it will pass away.

When I was a child, I spoke like a child, I thought like a child, I reasoned like a child; when I became a man, I gave up childish ways.

For now we see in a mirror dimly, but then face to face. Now I know in part; then I shall understand fully, even as I have been fully understood.

So faith, hope, charity abide, these three; but the greatest of these is charity.

It seems to me that the writer on charity has three possible excuses for embarking on the subject: the first, that Paul has left something out. But though he could hardly be speaking more concisely, and his words fill only one chapter in the letter he was writing to the Corinthians, it is hard to think of anything he has omitted. Yes, one could go on about some things - and to tell the truth, that is what I am planning to do. We must remember also that this was just part of one letter. He had many other things to tell them, including the schoolmasterly reproaches he addresses to them at the beginning, about Christian callings being different but all forming part of the body of Christ, and a great deal about the second coming, and how it should affect their lives. But it seems that he was inspired in this particular part of his letter. This was not necessarily something all of which they would understand when they heard it read out. He is speaking to all men and women and all nations; and there is nothing in what he says that can be faulted.

The second excuse is that what he is saying needs to be brought up to date. He was writing, after all, to a very new community of Christians who had much to learn, one that was very much on his mind, since he addressed at least two letters to them, but one which seems to have given him more trouble than the others combined. One need only compare this letter with those he wrote to the Philippians or Colossians to get the point.* But if one equates charity with kindness - and there is a case for doing so, though the two are by no means synonymous - one will find that nothing has changed. The world is still in as much need of kindness as it was in Paul's time. Probably more so.

Of course it is always difficult to compare the sum of human happiness or the reverse now with what was the case in the past. Too much has intervened. To start with, the population of the world has enormously increased, so that one would expect to find these same qualities increased in the same proportion. But the major change is that we are much more aware now of what is going on in the world than people were in Paul's time. The media have opened up for us the extent of the world's suffering. Every time we turn on the television or read a newspaper we are confronted with an image of war or starvation - the latter more often caused by incompetence or corruption of a brutal ruler than by natural causes. We see refugees either refused access to more prosperous countries or confined in the most barbarous of conditions. We see individuals persecuted or even killed by their own kinsmen... One could go on: the list is endless. And even closer at home, in one's individual life, one is aware of instances, if not of unkindness, at any rate of a lack of humanity; all of this makes one doubt if the world is getting any better. So, yes, it is dangerous to be drawn into comparisons. But there is nothing out of date in what Paul has to say on charity, no need to alter it in order to deal with our own conditions.

Finally, and this is the means which I intend to adopt, one can flesh out Paul's examples of charity and the need for it, by looking at the examples he gives and seeing what more can be said about them. Though I do not pretend for one moment to have the knowledge or the eloquence which he possessed, it is almost as if he had been asked to write a book rather than confine himself to a letter. And bearing in mind the disclaimers I have already given, I hope that nothing I say in what follows will be contrary to his sense or would have met with his disapproval.

There is another factor which comes into play, which may or may not be applicable to this chapter from 1 Corinthians. It sometimes happens that one is so familiar with a passage, so swayed by its beauty, that one is lulled into ignoring its meaning. I know that this happens to me with passages from scripture that I have heard so often that my mind, as it were, switches off when they start being read out. There is nothing deliberate about such a process. I do not close my ears to such a passage. Sometimes I am carried along to such an extent by the words that I feel I would like to say them in unison with the reader. Or sometimes the reading comes to an end and I realise that I have not heard a word of it and could not for the life of me repeat its meaning.

Nor is this confined to the scriptures. It can apply to poetry as well. I know for instance, the opening words of T S Eliot's *The Waste Land*

> April is the cruellest month, breeding
> Lilacs out of the dead land, mixing
> Memory and desire, stirring
> Dull roots with spring rain

so well that it was only when I was leading a small group in an analysis of the poem that I was forced to consider their meaning. Yes, of course, this goes in direct contradiction to everything one has thought about April. It is the time of renewal, the time, as Chaucer says, when 'smale fowles maken melodye'. Why on earth should it affect Eliot in this way? What is it that causes him to label it as the 'cruellest' month? And so on. This sort of unwilling amnesia may not affect readers who have gone this far with regard to the passage from the Corinthians since I have deliberately chosen, for its comparative unfamiliarity, at least for those brought up on modern translations, a version from the Revised Standard Version, which closely approximates to the beloved King James version. All I have done is to take the latter word 'charity' in place of 'love' as giving greater emphasis to the special quality demanded of Christians. But it may be that even the version I have given is so familiar to some that they have not taken in what it is saying. They have nodded their heads in agreement when they have heard it read out in church or at marriages, confident that they know all about it. But it may be that, like my own reaction to *The Waste Land*, they are deceiving themselves and require further elucidation.

Such, at any rate, are my motives for writing this book. I shall carefully study Paul's chapter in 1 Corinthians, often concentrating on one single word or phrase to see if one can further elucidate its meaning. But I shall also add some chapters of my own, whose purpose is to show how the modern Christian should react to Paul's scheme of charity and what part it should play in his life. This is not, as I say, because Paul is in any way out of date: it is strictly because circumstances change. The Church itself has altered out of all recognition from what it was in Paul's day: it is, for instance, much more structured, and presents us with a body of doctrine which may have existed in embryo at the time, but had yet to be defined. The problems with which Paul was concerned, at least in these letters, were those that confronted him when dealing with his difficult body of Corinthians. We are lucky that he has broken off from such concerns to leave us with this wonderful chapter which contains virtually the whole of the Christian message. In so doing he has left us a model of charity, a model so demanding that one can think it applies to anybody but oneself. He does not tell us how to attain it, though, by taking snippets from all his epistles, one could gain a pretty good idea of the code he thought should be followed by a true follower of the gospel.

Once again, this book is primarily intended for Christians, although it may also interest those who, while belonging to no faith and having perhaps an erroneously hostile attitude towards St Paul, nevertheless regard charity as the supreme virtue and would like to see more of it in their own lives and in the world as a whole. And though I have not always followed the idiom of inclusive language, it goes without saying that it is meant for men and women alike.

Note

*Some have questioned whether these letters belong to the Pauline canon.

1. THE CALL TO CHARITY

As I have already stated, few of the Corinthians could have been expected to take in the essence of the message which Paul was writing about in this chapter of his letter. They were, for the most part, uneducated men, prone to squabbles and difficult to teach. We know, moreover, from Acts that the bulk of the apostles' teaching - and Paul considered himself one of them - was that Jesus was the Messiah promised by God - thus in a way the fulfilment of the Jewish religion - that he had gone about doing good and performing miraculous cures, that he had finally been put to death, and that he had risen again. This last statement was the crux of their teaching: it explains, for instance, why the Athenians, who had listened up to this point, were so scornful of the new religion; and Paul makes it even plainer in this same letter to the Corinthians (15:14) when he says 'If Christ has not been raised, then our preaching is in vain and your faith is in vain'. This, then, was the message which the Corinthians were expected to take in.

It must not be forgotten that, though summaries of Jesus' teaching may have been available before this date, the gospels had not yet been written at the time Paul was preaching. All that we now know of Christianity as the religion of love and forgiveness could well have been a mystery to the Corinthians - it does not sound, at any rate, although this may have been part of his message, that they had taken it in very deeply - and Paul's chief concern is to stop them squabbling among themselves and claiming that there were different versions of the gospel depending on who was preaching it to them. If this makes them sound like infants, that is because they were, certainly compared to others among whom Paul was spreading the message.

I hinted in my introduction that it was by means of a special quality - and where it comes from we cannot be certain - that we are able to perceive the full force of what Paul is saying in that chapter of Corinthians. But most of us lack that special quality. We realise that a certain degree of charity is needed if we are to fulfil our calling as Christians; but we practise that degree sporadically, and, it would seem, regard our status as Christians as sufficient, if not to bypass the pains of purgatory, at any rate to save us from hell. There is a story told in *The Brothers Karamazov* of a woman condemned to hell because she has never done a good deed in her life. But no, she recalls, she once gave an onion to a starving beggar: surely that should be enough to save her. So she is given the chance of a reprieve. If she can haul herself upwards clinging to that onion alone, she will be spared hell and find salvation for her soul. So she tugs and tugs; but just as she is tugging, all the other souls in hell attach themselves to her and start tugging too. Angrily she kicks them off - and immediately falls into hell again. I may have got the details of the story wrong, but the point is clear enough (even if we have not got it already from the parable of Dives and Lazarus): it is by charity, and charity alone, that we shall be saved. Our church membership is in a sense irrelevant. We run the risk of being people who say after death 'Lord, lord' (Matt 7:21) but he does not recognise us. It is not, in other words, membership of a church alone that will guarantee us a place in heaven: it is how we behave as members of that church, above all whether we have practised the virtue of charity.

So what reaction should be expected from the person who reads or listens to this passage in the present century? Probably if he is reading it will evoke a more positive response: for reading is a voluntary act, and it implies that he is seeking to deepen his knowledge from it, possibly to see how it affects his life. But if he is listening to it, be it in a church or elsewhere, he is likely to have one of three different reactions. One, which I have already described, is of the person who knows it all, who could possibly recite the passage by heart, who is swayed by its music and beauty. In fact, so swayed is he by these emotions that he may miss its meaning altogether, he will just think that it is any old piece of prose which has its enduring appeal, but that is all.

A second is that of the person who partly takes in its meaning. I am not quite sure where he would figure in the parable of the sower and the seed. He recognises that charity is required of the Christian, and probably he will wish that he had been more charitable in the past. He may even recall some occasion when he has let fly some angry words, or failed to apologise to someone he has offended. 'Yes I will try to be more charitable in the future,' he will say with a sigh, and comforted by his good intention, he will kiss the bride and tuck into the champagne if it is a wedding. But when the next occasion comes round, and he hears the piece for the second time, his reaction will be much the same. He will have made some effort to improve himself in the meantime. He will restrain his tongue and look more favourably on his neighbour. But - and this is the reaction which will affect most of us - he will remain semi-committed. His charity is something he puts on when he remembers: it will not be a constant affair in his life. Sometimes it will inconvenience him, making him realise that if he were not a Christian, he would not have taken this path. But still it remains a quality that he puts on at will, that is not deeply embedded in him: and this, as I say, is where most of us reside.

But there is another response possible, though it will affect but a few, and here, at least, we can say with confidence where it belongs in the parable I have mentioned. Those who react in this way will be those who bring forth grain, some a hundredfold, some sixty, some thirty. The words that they have just read or heard will go deep into their soul, and henceforth life will never be the same. Even if they have heard them a hundred times before - and it need not be the reading from Corinthians on

8

which I am focusing, it may be something totally banal, something which seems irrelevant to any matter of religion or charity - that suddenly affects them in the way it has never done before. It is as if it has hit them for the first time: and we call this experience the moment of conversion.

Although there are classic cases of conversion within the Catholic church, the most notable being those of St Paul and St Augustine, the one I want to concentrate on is that of St Francis of Assisi because it suits my argument better. He was a rich young man who had never seriously devoted himself to the things of the Church, though he had had several intimations from God beforehand. One day, praying in the ruined chapel of San Damiano, just outside Assisi, he heard a voice saying 'Go, Francis, and repair my house which, as you see, is almost in ruins'. At first he misinterpreted these words, taking them as a command to repair the church he was in, but it was only later that their full import became apparent. The words themselves are of little consequence: they may even have arisen from his own subconscious. What matters is that he heard them and interpreted them after his fashion. Neither he, nor the Church, was ever the same again.

I said earlier that the source of this conversion is a mystery. The easy answer is to say that it comes from God and leave it at that. This, at any rate, exonerates those of us who do not get that far, who think it is well beyond our means. But there are two things wrong with that. One is that a response on the part of the individual is an indispensable part of the process - else why do we give the saints so much honour? Why, above all, do we revere the Virgin Mary for giving her consent to the angel's message when, presumably, it lay in her power to say no? That, after all, is what free will is about. We are always free to accept or to reject the gifts which God puts within our grasp, and amid all this call to sanctity there may well be some who turned it down, who were afraid of what it would bring, and preferred the rut in which they were living their lives. There is even a parable to this effect in Matthew 25: 14, that of the talents, and we sometimes find the treatment meted out to the third individual unfair, though it is in keeping with God's command that we should use the talents given us to the full. And the second is that the call to which the saints responded did not come out of the blue: I maybe have offended some by my statement that perhaps the words Francis heard arose from his subconscious. But we are certainly justified in thinking that the conversion of all the saints was preceded by anxious thought on their own part.

It lies in our power to imitate the saints. This is not to say that we should be exactly like them. Francis of Assisi was an individual person; if then we think of saints as people wholly remote from us, people whose sole function is to receive our prayers, to be revered, and to intercede for us, we are sadly mistaken. But we are equally mistaken if we think we should strive to imitate them to the letter, that there is no other way of being saints than that which they chose.

Thérèse of Lisieux taught us this more than a hundred years ago when, it might almost be said, she revolutionised the idea of sanctity. It was her wish to be a great saint, and she felt within herself the capacity to be a warrior, priest, apostle, doctor and martyr. Even towards the end of her life, when sickening with the tuberculosis which eventually killed her, she would have liked to have gone to Indochina as a missionary; but instead made it her duty to pray for, and advise, a young priest who was destined there. But for all her ambitions there was a very realistic side to her. She perceived that she had been called to the conventual life, and that it was within this convent that she was to fulfil her vocation. There was nothing spectacular about what she was called to do. Indeed many of her sisters considered her just an ordinary kind of nun, and were surprised when the question of her beatification came up.

The lesson, then, to be learnt from her life is that we are called to be ourselves, that there is no other pattern of sanctity we are called upon to adopt. We may pray to be like St Paul, St Augustine, St Francis; but if we are doing so we are making a great mistake. There is only one kind of saint we are meant to be, and that is ourselves.

This is the start of the spiritual life, and it may be its most humbling part. Many of us dream of escaping the unglamorous routines of our daily life and being transformed into something grand and heroic. It is, in fact, the illusion of those about to go on holiday. We dream that a change in surroundings will accomplish a change in ourselves, we shall leave behind all that we found boring or disagreeable, including the fact of being ourselves. But very soon, within a day or two, we find that this is not so. We are exactly the same person we have left behind. There may be new things to do, new sights to see, but our essential nature remains unchanged. This can be a great disillusionment, and explains why holidays do not always turn out to be the wonderful experiences we should like them to be.

Allied to this, for it is also a state of illusion, though a different kind altogether, is the fear that once having made such a big commitment, God is going to demand of us something well beyond our strength, something we find recorded in the lives of the saints we most admire, who were called, in certain cases, to leave home and property and adopt a completely new way of life. This, incidentally, is one of the signs of the difference between saints of today and those normally drawn up to be our models. I am writing this book mainly for the laity. But one of the things that strikes us when we consider the history of the saints throughout the ages is how few were drawn from that condition. How few in fact were married, how many were drawn from the religious life or the clergy, which gave them, in some respects, a certain freedom. Not the freedom to do as they liked - we rightly consider them as constrained in that respect - but at least the freedom to turn their lives round, not to fear for their families if they were called upon to begin again and found a new order. A different class of saint altogether is Jean Vianney, the curé d'Ars, who was not summoned to a new life, but who spent all his days as a parish priest, conscientiously performing his duties, to the extent that he was thoroughly exhausted by them and sometimes tried to escape from it all.

I called the process of conversion a humbling one, and so it is, for gradually, as we come to know God better, we are forced to give up our illusions and confront ourselves as we really are. Nobody likes doing this; and in addition there may be aspects of our personality which we would rather not face, which cause us shame, and, indeed, which we are now facing for the first time.

One of the major lessons we learn is the disadvantage it puts us in regard to other people. I said earlier that we need not fear having to give up our life and adopt something entirely new. This is not completely true. We are not circumscribed as are, perhaps, those who have been ordained or those in religious orders, but we will most definitely find ourselves circumscribed even if nothing around us has changed. I mean that we have set about a completely new life, one which involves, in St Paul's words, no boasting, or arrogance, or insisting on our own way. But others with whom we may be in contact are not so constrained. It is not that they are in any way evil, or committed to a way of life which we should regard as sinful. But they are still free to go their own way; and so, when dealing with them - and this applies to dealing with everyone we meet - we may feel at a distinct disadvantage. Something has dropped from us which gives other people the protection we no longer have. In the old days we could rely in our dealings with the world on habits, on aspects of our personality which we were sure belonged to the real 'us'; but now we suddenly realise that these bits of us, while not necessarily sinful, are something we are compelled to give up. It is a bit like being a non-aggressor in a world of aggressors. The only way we could survive would be in pretending to be aggressors ourselves, in adopting the ways of life that others show; but this we are not allowed to do.

So what is it that God wishes us to do? It is to follow literally the exhortations listed in Paul's thirteenth chapter to the Corinthians. We are right not to take literally some of the things we find in the New Testament. When we read that we should take out our eye if it offends us we know that we are on metaphoric ground (which does not mean to say that there have never been fanatics who have taken this literally). But other parts of the New Testament we should take literally and this includes the command (Matt 5:48) that we should be perfect.

Above all, we should read most carefully, and then see how it applies to us, the description which Paul gives about charity. It is not some distant ideal, it is to be practised literally. And this does not mean a partial commitment: it is something to which we have to give the whole of ourselves, every hour of the day. This is why I talk of commitment: it is not something we can do half-heartedly when we feel like it. It is something that has to be practised unremittingly, with the same fervour and dedication Christians of old gave when they were determined to seek perfection through the paths of prayer.

This is why it need make no difference in our outward circumstances. Indeed, if we are expecting it to do so, it means we are maintaining the illusion that it is something destined to come in the future and not now. The terrifying thing about Christianity is that it is always about now. We can no more postpone it than we can postpone passing before the judgement seat of God when we die: and indeed Jesus has harsh words (Matt 8:19) for those who have more pressing things on their mind when half inclined to follow him.

It sounds from what I have said as if there is little difference between this process of conversion and what the evangelical experiences when he or she gives themselves wholly to God, and in return are assured that their sins are forgiven, and in certain cases that they are destined for heaven; and indeed there are similarities. But if we examine them more closely, we shall learn that there are also considerable differences. For a start, the person I have been discussing does not receive this assurance: if anything, he feels guiltier than ever for the false life he has been leading to this point, for the fact that he has taken so long to come to this process of conversion. And he is very far from thinking that he has been saved. In fact he may never think in these terms at all. Like most Christians, he will know that salvation is far from certain, that it depends to a large extent on how one lives one's life.

Secondly, the experience that the evangelical receives seems to come directly from God or the Holy Spirit to mark his own efforts: he believes, in other words, that it is something implanted in him from outside. The process of conversion at which we have been looking may indeed start with God: it is God who has put it into the convert's heart to abandon his former life and to give all his efforts to charity. But it may not seem that way to him. With one portion of his soul he may be grateful to God for the blessing he has received; but it is more likely to seem the end of a long wrestle with his conscience, something, in fact, that he has worked out for himself. He feels, in other words, no sense of this being an experience which has come from the outside; and, allied with this, he will not see it as a mark of God's favour, in other words, a notable end. If anything, it is merely a beginning, and he may well find himself daunted by the task ahead.

But it is in a way a sort of end. He knows that he has to give up his previous life and that from now on something new is required of him. From this point onwards every moment of his life has to be devoted to charity. He can no longer choose: he has already made his choice. That said, there will be many moments of wrong choice, of failure to live up to the ideal that he has set himself. He may well find himself wrestling with his conscience all over again:

in these circumstances was it possible for him to do more? Has he missed an opportunity and followed his own will when he should have been looking for a chance to do someone a good favour? The beginning of the spiritual life, in particular, is a period racked with doubt. We never seem to have done enough; there is no conviction that God is satisfied with our efforts. Indeed, this is the time when we come closest to feeling that we are 'unprofitable servants', quite unworthy to stand in our Lord's presence.

And this is to be expected. For if God were to be always with us, that is to say were always to make his presence felt, there would be no inducement for us to progress. As it is, by withdrawing himself from us or at least by not showing that he is there, he always leaves us one step behind, never satisfied with our efforts, always anxious to do more.

One might think that this is something that arises only at the start of the spiritual life, that when we are safely ensconced on its plateaux there will be a period of ease, when we can sit back and bask in contentment of our efforts. And indeed such periods do come, but we must not make too much of them. God is always giving us something to do; and to remain still in the spiritual life is to go backwards. So we should be grateful when our efforts are rewarded, when we feel God's favour on us; but probably, paradoxically, he is most with us when he is absent, when we do not feel the sun of his favour shining on us.

I said that this is an experience which comes at every stage of the spiritual life, and it shows the part that patience plays in it, that we must always be patient even when things do not seem to be going our way. There is a beautiful poem by Gerard Manley Hopkins which illustrates this. Hopkins had a more disturbed spiritual life than most, as anyone who has read the 'terrible' sonnets written at the end of his life must know. He was literally terrified of God, when all we are encouraged to do is have fear of God. That is to say to assign him his rightful place as our creator, and to see ourselves as vastly inferior to him, as his creatures. But with Hopkins it seems to have gone beyond this. In *The Wreck of the Deutschland,* for instance, the poem that resurrected his career as a poet, this terror of God is translated, in the last line, into a physical image that projects a more nightmarish view of God than even the last sonnets do:

Thou knowest the walls, altar and hour and night:
The swoon of a heart that the sweep and the hurl of thee
 trod
Hard down with a horror of height:
And the midriff astrain with leaning of, laced with fire of
 stress.

There is another poem, written in 1879, in which he praises the virtues of patience.

When will you ever, Peace, wild wooddove, shy wings
 shut,
Your round me roaming end, and under be my boughs?
When, when, Peace, will you, Peace? I'll not play
 hypocrite
To own my heart: I yield you do come sometimes; but
That piecemeal peace is poor peace. What pure peace
 allows
Alarms of wars, the daunting wars, the death of it?

O surely, reaving Peace, my Lord should leave in lieu
Some good! And so he does leave Patience exquisite,
That plumes to Peace thereafter. And when Peace here
 does house
He comes with work to do, he does not come to coo,
He comes to brood and sit.

This is not the patience we are called upon to show to our friends and neighbours, and which comes high on St Paul's list. It is a patience which we have to develop towards ourselves, forgiving ourselves, if that is possible, for our many lapses, for our failure to live up to the image we have formed of ourselves. For it is certain that God forgives us, and we should learn to forgive ourselves. God does not expect perfection all at once from us. Indeed, perfection lies a long way ahead, and we have all sorts of obstacles to confront before we get there. And even if, by unremitting effort, we do succeed in getting somewhere near there, the need for patience will remain. For things will not always turn out as we should like them to; for much of the time we shall feel ourselves on our own, not totally abandoned, as we sometimes feel in the dark night of the spirit, when all hope seems lost and God is wholly absent, but still, much of the time, left to confront the world on our own.

Some, most notably Saints Paul and Teresa of Avila, say that, once they have reached the end of their efforts, the only consolation they could receive is to be united with Christ in death. Paul, for instance, says (Phil 1:23-4)

I am hard pressed between the two. My desire is to depart and be with Christ, for that is far better. But to remain in the flesh is more necessary on your account.

But I do not think this is likely to affect the lay person who is, at one and the same time, less inclined to spend time over prayer and less drawn towards introversion than one who is very conscious of God's presences and absences. Nor, incidentally, whatever he says about his longing to be with Christ in the passage above, did it stop Paul from preaching the gospel and attending to the task of his many churches; while Teresa, always a model of good sense, regarded the ideal life as combining the virtues of Mary and Martha. The lay person is more drawn towards action than contemplation; and for that reason such people will always find in life sufficient to engage their energies even when the time for maximum effort is past.

2.CHARITY AND PRAYER

Before moving on to the starting theme of this book, a close examination of Paul's words in 1 Corinthians 13, we should briefly consider the links between charity and prayer.

Prayer has always been regarded as an essential element in the life of a Christian, and so it is. We cannot progress without prayer. At the same time it is necessary to consider the role of prayer, and how it assumes different levels of importance at different stages of the spiritual life.

The main purpose of prayer may be said to be worship of God and thanks to him for the extraordinary gifts with which he has surrounded us, most notably the gift of life. But this was not how the great masters of prayer in the Catholic Church - Saints Teresa and John of the Cross, to name but two examples - saw it. To them it was a weapon, a definite means, of the advancement towards God; and this is how the souls determined to progress to the limits of perfection saw it. True, the other aspects of prayer were, in their eyes, never to be neglected, but Teresa, for instance, gives pride of place to self-examination, and to the way in which it can correct faults and lead the soul on a closer path to God.

Nowadays that is not the way in which we would look at it. There is no agreed account of the role that prayer should play in a lay Christian's life. We are constantly encouraged to pray, but with no certainty about its aims beyond the obvious one of intercession. Jesus gave us the Lord's Prayer, which covers most of what we should dwell on in prayer, and also taught us about its urgency. In two parables in particular (Luke 11:5, Luke 18:2) he stresses this need, and he reinforces it in Matthew 7:7. On the other hand he spent long nights in solitary prayer with the Father and we cannot imagine that was spent solely in petition. In other words there are different forms of prayer, and in his teaching at least Jesus seems to have stressed the role of petition.

Nowadays we should regard the person who is praying only for himself, and dwelling on his needs, as selfish. We should expect him to grow out of this form of prayer as he becomes more aware of the world outside. And certainly at this moment there is a great deal to pray about as regards intercession. As I write, the world is devastated with a deadly new virus which means that we are in total lockdown; and so our prayers go towards those who are affected by this virus and their loved ones; but they certainly also include those working to reduce it, the front line staff who daily put themselves in danger for the sake of others, the scientists working on a cure, and those who go about their normal duties in this time of crisis: postmen, dustmen, those working in food shops and so on.

But even if this new plague were not upon us we should have plenty to pray about: our families, our friends, particularly those who are in need, the Church, the cessation of wars, the sick, the lonely, prisoners, the unemployed…The list is endless, which is why we should try not to let ourselves be engulfed by all that we feel required of us, but instead devise a plan, devote a good deal of our prayer to the needs of the world, but pray for them rationally, in order, and not attempt to take them all in at one go.

Adoration is probably the hardest part of prayer for the human mind to engage in. But we have the Lord's Prayer which encompasses all our needs. It is hard to think of a better way to start off prayer. God is 'hallowed' in it, which seems to satisfy this important requirement of prayer. It is followed by something probably regarded as just as essential, something which we may indeed consider the whole purpose of why we are engaged in prayer. It is where we ask to be rid of our faults, and to become more like God in character. It is impossible to lay down how long we should spend on this aspect of prayer. Some, already convinced of their faults, and determined to put them right, may spend less time on it than others. Others, less ready to embrace God, will take longer. But for all it is important to stress that length is not the essential part of prayer. We *all* of us, when we have finished praying, think that we could have spent longer on it, that we have not said enough. This is because at no point does God descend and say 'Well done, thou good and faithful servant'. We have to reconcile ourself to the fact that God is largely absent from our prayer in the early stage of our lives. We are lucky if he gives us an insight into the next step ahead of us, or what it is that particularly calls for amendment, something with maybe has never occurred to us before.

I spoke earlier of patience, and never is patience needed more than in the early stages of prayer. It is hard to get onto one's knees every day, or whatever position we care to adopt, and to reconcile ourselves to the fact that nothing dramatic is likely to happen. The work is all on our side at this time, and any rewards that come to us are more likely to be the products of our own imaginations, particularly when they are working overtime in our search for God, than anything that genuinely comes from him.

Where, however, we can make progress is in our pursuit of charity. Whatever frustration we may feel about the way our prayer is going, we are free to act. A curious blindness sometimes comes over us about this. We rise from prayer and think 'Am I getting better? Well that was not a very satisfactory experience, I am still far away from God.' But we can at least make it a more satisfactory experience by the way we act. Everybody, whether converted or not, at whatever stage of prayer they may find themselves, is free to turn his actions more in the direction of others than towards himself, and so to please God. As I say, we sometimes forget this. We think that all has to be accomplished by prayer when, even if we do not pray at all, or at least pray only perfunctorily, we are still capable of turning our minds in the direction of charity.

Some Christians, however, may already be convinced that this is the path to follow. They have, as it were, already undergone a type of conversion. True, there are still many faults to put right in their character, some of which they may not at this stage even be aware of, but they are already capable of embarking on what Paul regards as the most important of the virtues, that which gives the title to this book.

Others lack what I can only call imagination. They cling stubbornly to prayer and think that nothing can be accomplished until they succeed in that medium. And still others are not yet convinced that charity is the path to God. They struggle with themselves, are reluctant to let go. There are too many things of this world to which they are attached: it may be love of money, an adulterous relationship, or simply fear of what God may demand from them. All of these things are very well described in Francis Thompson's poem *The Hound of Heaven.* And so for them the process will very likely be longer until they realise that charity answers all their needs and the requirements of God.

So what is this charity we are talking about, something of which we have spoken so far in very abstract terms? It may involve no more than spending time with one's children and really listening to what they have to say. It may involve seeking out some way of giving pleasure to one's husband or wife instead of sinking into an unproductive routine leading to the thought that there is no way this marriage can be improved. It may involve at least speaking to the seller of the Big Issue, whose eye one had previously desperately striven not to catch, even if one does not buy his paper. It may take the form of a kindly word to a colleague at work whom one had previously neglected, even a suggestion of lunch together. It may consist of putting a bit more into the weekly collection at church or responding to one of the numerous appeals that daily come through one's letter box. There are countless acts one can do which take up very little of one's time before one comes onto the greater works of charity, and which seem never to have entered one's head until this second.

These are small things, and they may not appear at first sight to make much difference. But they are a start and can convince one that there are other ways of pleasing God than through prayer alone. But of course prayer is still vital, and one neglects it at one's peril. For a start commitment is likely to be still weak at this stage, and requires constant reinforcing. It is all too easy to think that, because one has adopted one form of action that involves charity, the path of full union with God lies clear ahead. Or one can get distracted and fall back into one's old way of living. Prayer is thus a way of keeping one in the right direction; but it also opens up new ways of pursuing this path to charity which is to be one's new life. Sometimes these new ways strike one as a sort of revelation, and one is amazed that one hasn't thought of them before. They involve perhaps resuming contact with an old friend one has neglected, or breaking some stupid habit at work which before this had seemed irrevocable. And prayer reveals more and more hidden aspects of one's character, things which had not been seen as faults before, or at least not definite faults, things that at any rate prevented one from giving one's full attention to God.

It is impossible to say how long this period of action reinforced with prayer will last. For a start it depends on the age at which one takes it up and the degree of one's commitment. It is likely, for instance, that an older person, possibly a widow or widower, who previously had found satisfaction in the things of the world, will, disillusioned, turn to God and find the way back to him quite easily. Or there may be younger people with initially good intentions who, nonetheless, have their lives to live and so forget about God for a time. It is sometimes thought that God works independently of time and of all other things that occur in one's life. But this is not so, and the timing of the sacraments - confirmation, for instance, coming at a vital time in one's life, when one is entering adulthood for the first time - shows this. It is a cliché to say that God works in a mysterious way, but we should also think of him working very closely with the demands of nature. After all, it is a major affirmation of our Christian life that he loves us: and so, just as a good parent will match their treatment to the age their son or daughter has reached, so God will take infinite pains not to do something which breaks into our normal life too intensely, but will seem part of the natural pattern of things.

Neither Teresa nor John of the Cross will commit themselves to how long this service of God without apparent reward will last; though John expects contemplation, or the direct experience, of God to follow quite early on in the life of the committed monastic. Teresa is much more aware of the temptations along the way, of how one may fall back, or never indeed reach one's full potential as a Christian. Such reservations, and more, lie in the path of the lay Christian who has every incentive, even if he knows where his rightful duty lies, to ignore it and to become distracted by the many other things on his plate. So that one can safely agree with John, that the determining factor is commitment. And provided this commitment is real and strong, there may come, after one has persevered with charity and the way of perfection, an experience which Teresa has incomparably described in *The Interior Castle V:1:* 'God implants himself in the interior of that soul in such a way that, when it returns to itself, it cannot possibly doubt that God has been in it and it has been in God; so firmly does this truth remain in it that, although for years God may never grant it that favour again, it can never quite forget it nor doubt that it has received it.' Or it may be by some other method that God shows himself to the soul and assures it of his existence.

But it is worth dwelling on the last words of Teresa's description. For it is not God's purpose to turn the lay person into an exact replica of the contemplative for whom Teresa was primarily writing. He wants such a soul to pursue its way in the world he has created, to persist in charity and above all in its relations with those about him. So - and though the process may be extremely painful, to strive after a repetition of this close intimacy with God, and gradually to realise that it will not be repeated, that the world about one has not changed - this is the reality, and the lay person realises more and more that he is called to charity and that is all that matters.

Prayer after such a direct experience of God is bound to change, and becomes more a focus of adoration and thanksgiving than of earnestly seeking to do God's will and wrestling with the problems that come in the way of spiritual progress. But it is also fair to say that prayer from this stage becomes harder, that one lacks the words that would express one's relation with God and wants solely to be with him in a state of union. One may - and this is really the desirable position to find oneself in - be in a state of constant prayer, when words and set times do not come into it, when one is often shorn of words at the times one has set aside for prayer. But that does not mean that one is not praying. The desirable thing is to be constantly in the presence of God. Words, in fact, do not matter; and it is very tempting to say, something which will be discussed in a later chapter, that formal periods of prayer are at this stage unimportant, that charity itself is a means of communication with God and is thus an adequate means of prayer.

In a way, then, the lay person is better prepared than the contemplative (and most contemplatives are to be found in religious orders) for what follows, the apparent disappearance from one's life of God, the sense that one has totally lost his favour and will never regain it, in what is called the dark night of the spirit. For though nothing is as severe as this, the lay person's whole life has been spent in *not* knowing God, whereas the contemplative's life, so well described by Teresa, has been spent in alternate periods of *knowing* God, of being linked in an intimate relationship with him, and then finding to his or her dismay that the relationship apparently disappears, and that all one can do is long for its return.

This is not to say that more lay people enter the final stage of the spiritual life - the dark night of the spirit - which leads to union with God, than those whose life is given over to contemplation. On the contrary, and there seem to be a number of reasons for this. One, that the lay life was for a long time considered inferior to that spent in the monastery and convent: and thus lay people were not properly taught the rudiments of the spiritual life. In other words, they had no sort of knowledge that they could climb so high, and so were reconciled to the fact that their life would always be spent in the thankless task of doing what is expected of a Christian, with all the thanks reserved for the time when one's earthly life is over.

And the other reason is that the enclosed life is definitely more favourable to the desired end, namely union with God. It is, for a start, calmer: the monk or nun has more time to reflect on what he or she is doing, and has more support from the community. And thus worldly cares, with their many surprises, have a way of keeping apart from the religious community. The lay person is constantly at the mercy of these shocks and surprises and so is more inclined to lose his way, to be distracted, or simply overwhelmed by the vicissitudes of life. In other words, more people from religious communities, proportionately, at present come to the full knowledge of God; but this may alter as an increasing number of lay people get instructed in the spiritual life and learn that they too are capable of perfection.

As with the period before direct experience of God becomes possible, so one cannot say how long this period of comparative felicity will last before it gives way to darkness and the apparent loss of God, in the dark night of the spirit. Much will depend on the willingness of the person concerned to go through with it, to realise that he must not take for granted the favours he has been given. And it would also depend most strongly - a decision which it is really for God, not the individual to make - on who is capable of going through with it. For the dark night of the spirit is undoubtedly a testing and difficult time to go through. It seems a reversal of all that one has previously learnt, that God is a loving father and will always be with one. On the contrary he now seems, if not totally absent, malevolent, not in the least bit interested in one, so that the individual has no hope of ever emerging from this state or being guaranteed a place in heaven.

It is no use downplaying the torments of the dark night of the spirit, as indeed Ruth Burrows tends to do in *Guidelines for Mystical Prayer,* seeing it as something which John of the Cross exaggerates, possibly as a result of his cruel imprisonment. Sooner or later we must all come to it. For John clearly says (*The Dark Night of the Soul* 11.XX.5) that those who accomplish it on earth are spared the pain of purgatory. And conversely, purgatory is a place, or state, where the pains of the dark night are accomplished in a different way. One is again separated from God, and uncertain how long this punishment will last (it is in any case futile to talk of time as we experience it, in the concept of life after death. Eternity, or even the measurement of time by months and days, have no real meaning in God's kingdom. We continue to think of them in these terms, and use such things as indulgences to lessen the periods souls spend in purgatory; but we have no real knowledge of how God measures time, and whether such things as being allowed to see God face to face, or its reverse, damnation, are not instantaneous experiences rather than things which we can measure in our own time).

But this is to anticipate. What can be said with certainty is that the period following one's first direct experience of God is one of ease; and the person who has entered it will be disturbed by much less of a moral struggle. He knows that God is always at hand to forgive him the little sins into which he is bound to fall; while anything more serious requires as usual the help of the confessional. But all who enter it - even for those in whom, in accordance with

Teresa's words, this is a one-off gift, not to be repeated - life will never be the same. He feels a new freedom about all he does; what before would have involved a moral struggle now appears second nature to him; and it is for this reason that he can never imagine that still more will be required of him, that this is not the end of the road and that he had better not wish to cling to this oasis for ever.

Probably enough time has been spend on the dark night of the spirit, though it is worth saying a bit more about it since it is likely to be the hardest part of the spiritual ladder which the Christian is called upon to climb. In any case, it is difficult to give precise guidance as to how to get through this stage in that it is entirely individual. The person concerned may have read dozens of accounts of the state, he may have total certainty about God's mercy, but, when it is experienced, it will still seem something reserved for him alone. Others may have got through it; others may have been saved; but he not. He is the exception to the rule: indeed he cannot conceive of any possible outcome except that he has lost God for ever.

John of the Cross stresses the importance of faith at this stage. Indeed, his whole output seems devoted to faith - one would guess that it is the most frequently recurring word in his prose works - to require that we should live by it rather than on any real or imagined manifestation of what God has in store for us. Teresa is slightly less strict in what it requires. She stresses that ordinary human activities - what she calls the role of Martha rather than that of Mary - can still be carried on at this stage, and that they provide relief. In other words, not to be obsessed by it, not to dwell on it, is part of the answer. And this applies particularly to the lay person who is, after all, very much involved in the processes of life, who cannot afford to give up the concentration he bestows on his family, his friends, his work. He may, in any case, not know what is happening to him, since, unless he is one of those whom Ruth Burrows (*Guidelines for Mystical Prayer,* chapter 5) calls as equipped with 'the light', he may not have much insight into his condition. For all, therefore, there is the requirement to carry on, not to forgo the path of charity on which they are embarked.

There is any case a certain proviso to be applied to John's words that faith is the only thing that will carry one through this dark night. For in a sense the choice has already been made. What can one do but follow the words Macbeth uses in a totally different context: 'Returning were as tedious as go o'er'? In other words, having got so far, it is doubtful whether the person concerned has any alternative but to continue. He may, of course, go completely off the rails, imagine that, since God no longer exists or is permanently dissatisfied with him, he may as well give himself over to all the pleasures he has previously forgone. Which it is why it is important that the Church should give continuous instruction on the possibilities of the spiritual life, should not leave the individual to flounder without guidance, should be in touch with the rich mystical tradition which it has inherited, and should always be at hand to help with teaching those who are determined not to be content with mediocrity, but to seek perfection in this world.

3. I CORINTHIANS 13: VERSES 1-2

It is time now to examine what Paul actually wrote.

The tongue of men and of angels

St Paul obviously did not have a very high opinion of his abilities as a speaker. He says as much in 2 Corinthians 11:6 when he states 'Even if I am unskilled in speaking, I am not in knowledge'. And he reinforces this in 10:10 when he imagines his audience saying 'His letters are weighty and strong, but his bodily presence is weak, and his speech of no account'. In both of these statements he may have been self-deprecatory, however. We learn from Acts 14 that at Lystra, when the people were inclined to treat the two apostles, Paul and Barnabas, as gods, they called Paul Hermes because he was the chief speaker. And certainly the speeches recorded by Luke in Acts seem to be carefully thought out and well chosen.

But we must remember that a historian of the time did not regard it as a duty to record what was actually said. He may not have been present on all occasions, and his words reflect more what he thinks should or would have been said rather than presenting us with a verbatim account. When all is said and done, however, it was by word of mouth that the gospel was spread. Paul may have addressed his congregations by letter, but only after a believing community was established - and we are indeed fortunate to have so many letters, the earliest New Testament documents. The normal pattern of events was to gather an assembly of Jews primarily, and, if they failed to respond to his message, Gentiles, and to try to persuade them by words.

It is likely then that Paul is saying no more than that, even if he had miraculous powers, but lacked charity, this would not avail him (it is noticeable that he keeps up this musical metaphor until the end). But the very fact that he starts his encomium on charity as the one Christian virtue which it is necessary for all to have with a section on speech possibly shows what an ordeal it was to get up in each new place in front of a new group of strangers and try to persuade them of the worth of his message.

Prophetic powers

Here, warming in on his message, he is being much more radical. Prophecy, as we learn in Romans 12:6, was, with service, teaching, exhortation, material and other aid, and acts of mercy, regarded as part of the normal activity required of Christian life. Such gifts could not be separated: the Christian community was a body, the Body of Christ, so it was wrong to prize any of these activities as independent of the others. Nevertheless, prophecies had been highly regarded before Jesus' time. The prophets were the people who did not necessarily foresee the future, in our modern use of the word, but who continually, and often with grumbling or at risk to themselves, as we learn from Jonah and Jeremiah, had to recall Israel to its duty of monotheism, to the fact that they owed all that they were to this one true God. It is not too much to say that they were the foundation upon which the whole Jewish religion depended: and their importance is shown in the account of the transfiguration when it is Moses and Elijah, the last as the representative of this great string of prophets, who appear at Christ's side.

All mysteries

Paul is very fond of the word 'secret' and uses it many times. More often than not it is used to express what was God's purpose from the beginning, but has only now been revealed through Jesus, and later through his apostles. It is in this sense that he uses it at the end of the letter to the Romans (16:25-26) when he says

Now to him who is able to strengthen you according to my gospel and the preaching of Jesus Christ, according to the revelation of the mystery which was kept secret for long ages but is now disclosed and through the prophetic writing is made known to all nations, according to the command of the eternal God, to bring about the obedience of faith - to the only wise God be glory for evermore through Jesus Christ! Amen.

It is also in this sense that Jesus uses it when he speaks of the truth having been revealed to babes and sucklings, and how God alone knows the time of the second coming (Acts 1:7).

Paul regarded himself as one of the apostles (1 Cor 15:8-9) though he had been called late - he speaks of himself as one 'untimely born' - and deserving to be called the least of the apostles because he persecuted the church of God. Nevertheless he had been granted a special vision of Jesus Christ; and his conversion had been brought about for the task of bringing the gospel to Gentiles as well as Jews, something that may have been foretold by the prophets, but would have been an unwelcome revelation to many of the Jews of his time. Ananias, for instance who restored Paul's sight (or Saul as he was known at the time) was told 'He is a chosen instrument of mine to carry my name before the Gentiles and kings and the sons of Israel' (Acts 9:15).

The apostles had frequently referred to the mystery of the second coming: but Paul was first to reveal this in detail:

Lo! I tell you a mystery. We shall not all sleep, but we shall all be changed in a moment, in the twinkling of an eye, at the last trumpet. For the trumpet will sound, and the dead will be raised imperishable, and we shall all be changed. 1 Cor 15:51-2

It is this version of the last day which has stuck in the minds of Christians and led to the belief that after death we shall be reunited with God as far as our souls are concerned, but shall have to wait for the last day - what Paul describes as the sound of the trumpet - to acquire our new, perfectly restored bodies.

Thus Paul was using the word in a variety of ways, but always referring to a truth previously kept secret by God but now, in these latter days, been made known to the world.

The modern Church, or at least part of it, uses the word in a slightly different sense, to describe things which cannot be perceived by the intellect alone, but demand faith. Among these is the doctrine of the Trinity - how can three persons possibly exist as a single entity? - and the transformation of the bread and wine into the body and blood of Christ - it tastes the same, looks the same and smells the same, doesn't it? Thus the priest in the Roman Catholic church asks the congregation to repent of their sins before celebrating 'the sacred mysteries'; and, in a more Pauline sense, the congregation acclaims immediately after the consecration, the 'mystery of faith', that Christ died for our sins, rose again, and will come a second time.

But there were two other uses which were current in Paul's time, and have never entirely passed away. Thus, at a time particularly of persecution, the essence of the faith might be kept hidden from all who were not privileged to partake of it; and it is interesting that the Orthodox church keeps something of this meaning in the affirmation which its adherents say immediately before receiving Holy Communion: 'I will not reveal your mystery to your adversaries.'

And another use with which Paul would certainly have been familiar - he may even have been having a dig at it when he talks of 'understanding all mysteries' - would have been the mystery religions in the East, and particularly the Eleusinian mysteries. These would have been celebrated all over the Roman empire by those, in particular, dissatisfied with Greek or Roman mythology, and looking for a truer form of religion. But knowledge in such mysteries proceeded by stages; and its full extent could only be revealed to the initiated. Gnosticism, which for a long time battled with mainstream Christianity, was rather similar: its doctrines or rites were considered secret except to the initiated.

It is likely that Paul, who uses the term mystery so often in his letters, was using it in the first of these senses, to refer to something known to God alone. Modern thinkers would demand an explanation for many things not known to Paul, such as, for instance, why the way quantum particles behave cannot be fitted into the general theory of relativity put forward by Einstein, and whether intelligent life exists on other planets. But if Paul was using it somewhat in this way, to mean all the secrets of the universe, it would be a synonym for the knowledge which immediately follows. So it seems natural to conclude that he was using the word in its religious sense.

All knowledge

At first sight this looks merely an intensification of what has gone before, and can be put in the same category, as a mere turn of phrase. But there is more to it than that. Paul was suspicious of knowledge that did not have as its end results a greater love and knowledge of God. Time and again he shows this: in 1 Corinthians 1: 22, for instance:

> For Jews demand signs and Greeks seek wisdom, but we preach Christ crucified, a stumbling block to Jews and folly to Gentiles, but to those who are called, both Jews and Greeks, Christ the power of God and the wisdom of God.

And again in Colossians 2:8 he says

> See to it that no one makes a prey of you by philosophy and empty deceit, according to human tradition, according to the elemental spirits of the universe and not according to Christ.

Incidentally it is notable how even in the first of these epistles cited, a comparatively early one, he makes no distinction between Jews and Greeks, who were the majority speakers of the empire. Although brought up as a Pharisee himself, and proud of his Pharisee tradition (Acts 22:3) he realised sooner than the other apostles - this is to assume that his conversion predated Peter's vision near the house of Cornelius - that the word of God was not confined to the Jews. It took a vision (Acts 10:9) for Peter, the chief of the apostles, to realise this. And this talk of mere intellectual cleverness as inferior, and in some ways hostile, to the cleverness of God, which has humility as its foundation, is thoroughly in keeping with Christ's saying in Luke 10:21 'I thank thee, Father, Lord of heaven and earth, that thou hast hidden these things from the wise and understanding, and revealed them to babes; yea, Father, for such was thy gracious will.' And he goes on to reinforce this by stating 'Unless you turn and become like children, you will never enter the kingdom of heaven.' It is worth noting, also, that he thoroughly perplexed Nicodemus (John 3) by telling him that, in order to see the kingdom of God, one must be born anew.

We witness too how, on the one occasion that Paul tried to flatter his audience and bring in a reference to their reputation (Acts 17:22), he was mocked and made no attempt to stay. The Athenians, certainly compared to the Corinthians, who gave Paul endless trouble, but had humility in their hearts, were clever-clever; and when Paul says, in the speech he gave to them, that they are 'very religious', he appears to be flattering them, but is really telling them off (the King James version has here that they are too 'superstitious').

We must remember that Paul himself was a highly educated man. No one brought up a Pharisee, 'educated according to the strict manner of the law of our fathers' (Acts 22:3), and sitting at the feet of Gamaliel*, could have failed to be so. He is therefore not railing against learning as such, but only the learning that seems to be wise it its own eyes, that is satisfied with itself and wholly opposed to the wisdom of Christ.

There is a danger, however - and particularly in the Roman Catholic church, which has always put a high premium on authority - of regarding the intellect as a dangerous quality, one which is more than capable of leading one astray (it is worth noting, in this regard, that is was for eating the fruit of the knowledge of good and evil that Adam and Eve were expelled from the garden). Whereas the intellect, like anything else that comes from God - creative ability, beauty, or the ability to run fast - is a gift and should be cultivated to the full. In the past the Catholic church has had its share of intellectuals - St Thomas Aquinas is but one example - but it has also been guilty of muzzling its theologians, of putting too great an emphasis on authority. For this the doctrine of infallibility is partly to blame. It is taken to mean that any form of disagreement with the Pope, whether or not he is speaking infallibly, is what amounts to a sin; whereas in fact infallibility belongs to very few of the Church's doctrines and apart from those which are written in stone, as it were, and contained in the creeds, it is generally agreed that they apply only to three of the dogmas that have been proclaimed in the last 200 years: infallibility itself, and the two dogmas relating to the Virgin Mary, her Immaculate Conception (not to be confused with the Virgin Birth) and her Assumption. But in all other areas theologians should be free to speculate; and their speculations, as to what properly belongs to Christian tradition and what does not, have been of great benefit to the Church over the ages.

Faith to move mountains

Jesus had used exactly the same image (Matt 17:20) when reproaching the disciples for their lack of faith. But the gospels had not been published at this time, and it is likely that Paul was simply using a phrase in common parlance at the time. He is here moving on to much more controversial territory, for faith, of course, is and was a

35

very desirable quality. It was what St Paul was trying to instil into those with whom he came into contact, and it was an enormously complicated thing, especially for the Corinthians, who could not be expected to understand, all in one go, how Christ, crucified as a common criminal, had risen from the dead; how from this moment they were to worship him and him alone; and how this was to affect their behaviour. Paul had experienced a moment of intimacy with Christ. He is not one of those of whom Jesus had said (John 20:29) 'Blessed are those who have not seen and yet believe'. His faith was complete; and it is even possible to say of him that he was granted a privilege not known to the eleven faithful apostles, who had, however, benefited from Christ's intimacy. They had been with Jesus from the beginning; they knew what he was like as a man, and had been utterly transformed by the news of his resurrection. But Paul was a late disciple, 'untimely born', and it was likely that he would have kept to the end of his life the knowledge that he was a sinner who had only been raised to his position by the special grace of God.

It is very hard for us to conceive of a faith which does not involve some sort of charity. But we must do our best to imagine it. An evangelical, for instance, satisfied that he has received from God a sign that his sins were forgiven and his place was now assured in heaven might - though I stress that it is hard to conceive - think that he had to do nothing more to earn his ultimate reward. Similarly, a Roman Catholic, satisfied that he had been born into, or found, the correct faith witnessed to by Jesus in Matthew 16:18, might imagine that this was all that was required of him. But a quick reading of the Scriptures would have told them both more. Jesus repudiates those (Matt 7:21) who expect their faith alone to save them, and in the rather frightening parable which occurs in the same gospel (25:31) he makes plain the things that a Christian is expected to do: feed the hungry, clothe the naked, and so on. Likewise Paul, in the passage which we are examining, stresses how important it is that we should alter our behaviour, embrace patience and kindness and all else that belongs to charity.

For a long time there was a somewhat arid controversy between the Catholic and Reformed churches about whether justification - that is, to be considered right in the sight of God - demanded good works to be done or was a matter of faith alone. I say arid because the matter has now largely been solved and turned out to depend on a misunderstanding of the term 'justification' which both parties were using. One of the texts on which Catholics depended was that found in the second chapter, verse 14, of the letter attributed to St James:

> What does it profit, my brethren, if a man says he has faith but has not works? Can his faith save him? If a brother or sister is ill-clad and in lack of daily food, and one of you says to them, "Go in peace, be warmed and filled." without giving them the things needed for the body, what does it profit?

This is no more than common sense, and is echoed in 1 John 4:20, in which we find the words

> If anyone says "I love God," and hates his brother, he is a liar, for he who does not love his brother whom he has seen, cannot love God whom he has not seen.

Paul is thus using an extreme case, which may perhaps have been put forward by Gnosticism, but would hardly be embraced by anyone today.

These are, however, strong words and we should heed them. Faith, like hope and love, has been designated since St Paul's time as one of the cardinal virtues. Yet Paul is quite clear that love - or charity as it is here called - surpasses the other two, and is the only one that will endure. For in the kingdom of heaven, as the hymn puts it, faith will vanish into sight, hope be emptied in delight; but love will be the very mode of our existence.

Note

* It was Gamaliel, incidentally, who gave the Sanhedrin the wise advice (Acts 5:34) that they should wait and see before dealing too harshly with the apostles: 'for if this plan or this undertaking is of men, it will fail; but if it is of God, you will not be able to overthrow them. You might even be found opposing God!'

4. VERSE 3

St Paul's last two examples of the vanity of actions performed without charity seem to demand a new chapter since they represent what many would regard as the height of that virtue. Jesus twice spoke in a way that is relevant to this theme: on the first occasion (Matt 19:16) it was to the young man who came to him asking what he had to do to inherit eternal life. Jesus told him that if he would be perfect, he had to sell all that he had, give to the poor, and follow him. But this he could not do since he had great possessions.

This presents us with two problems. Is this the only way to become perfect? For a long time it was thought so, and entry into a religious order was considered the only way to achieve it. But perhaps Jesus was talking specifically to the young man in his situation: at any rate one would like to think so. Perhaps perfection can also be achieved in other ways, particularly by the laity who, after all, are bound to preserve a certain amount of their money if only to attend to their children's wants. So although one recognises and admires those who take to the letter Christ's command, one would have hesitation in taking it as a general injunction.

The second occasion (Mark 12:42) came when he was observing those who were contributing to the treasury for the relief of the poor. 'Many rich people put in large sums. And a poor widow came, and put in two copper coins, which make a penny.' But she, Jesus says, has contributed more than the wealthy because they gave out of their abundance, whereas she had contributed all that she had.

Referring this lesson for a moment to myself, and I suspect to other Christians as well, I would not regard myself as particularly rich. I subscribe to a number of charities as well as giving what I regard as a fair amount to the weekly parish collection (though this does not amount to a tithe, or a tenth of my income, which certain churches demand of their members). I know that I could give more. Every now and then, for instance, leaflets turn up in my post asking for contributions to some particularly deserving cause. Just occasionally I respond to them, but more often than not I toss them away thinking that I have already done my bit (I have omitted to mention the fact that my contributions to the charities I support have hardly altered over the ages, so that what might have been regarded as a generous amount has certainly deteriorated over time). Am I alone in this, or is this how other Christians behave? We give - and Britain is one of the most generous of nations when it comes to donating to some emergency appeal, like response to an earthquake or starvation in a remote corner of the world. But we could do more. And probably most, like myself, are left with a feeling of guilt as we carelessly toss these appeals for our help into the recycling bin.

In my particular case I think the reason is a totally unreasonable fear of destitution which I should long ago have overcome. I have at various times of my life been without a job, and, though the time of this is long since past, I suppose it is an irrational fear that still possesses me that this could happen again and that I should be left on my own resources or, worse still, come begging to be readmitted to my parents' home (I still have dreams of this sort, and it is a great relief to wake up from them). So it is not entirely meanness which prevents me doing my share - and I suspect this applies to other Christians as well. It is more thoughtlessness, and a feeling that one cannot possibly respond to all the charities that require one's help. So it is safest not to think about them all that much, to respond when conscience gets the better of one, but otherwise to deal with the guilt that arises as best one may.

Paul is obviously not asking that we should give more. He is simply pointing out that contributing the most that he can possibly imagine will do us no good unless it is accompanied by charity, whose characteristics he will presently define. But I have a feeling that many of us consider that we have played our part once we have put our contribution in the church's plate, that this represents, say, 70% of what is required of us. It is, of course, generous to give what we can to the church and other causes, and we should never be ashamed of it; but we are sadly deluded if we think that this is all that Christianity is about. The widow, after all, gave very little; and yet, in Jesus' eyes, her gift was to be prized above those who have given more. It is easy to conceive of a person, say a down and out, who has nothing, not even the proverbial dime, to give. Is such a person to be considered unfit to pay his or her respects to God in church?

We are sometimes judged by the clothes we wear in church (this has happened to me once). Of course it is necessary to be respectfully dressed for the occasion. But within those limits I do not see that it has much importance. I admit that I should be slightly shocked if I were to see someone come into church dressed in filthy old rags, having made no effort to smarten himself up; but this says more about me than the person concerned. It is on a par with what Jesus says about food (Mark 7: 19). What goes into a man cannot defile him. It is what is stored in his heart, and then emerges, that is evil; and he goes on to list the things that come out of the heart: evil thoughts, fornication, theft, murder, adultery, coveting, wickedness, deceit, licentiousness, envy, slander, pride, foolishness. It is a pretty exhaustive list; and yet there are still things that one could add to it.

So much of our life is a craving for respectability: and it is in a church that we think we should show our best side. But God is not solely interested in our best side. He wants what we normally hide from others, the sins listed above, the things that really defile us. It is these things, things that we normally conceal from others, and possibly from ourselves as well, that he seeks to reform. And every time we put on a false facade it is harder for him to do so. For eventually we become convinced that we are what the facade represents, and that is when we are in deep trouble. The tax collector who beat his breast crying 'God, be merciful to me a sinner!' earned Jesus' praise far more than the Pharisee who thought that he had no need of God's mercy, and whose prayer, indeed, represented a list of his accomplishments.

We come now to what has generally been thought of as the most generous act of which an individual is capable, martyrdom. Jesus has said as much in John 15:13 :'Greater love hath no man than this, that a man lay down his life for his friends'. Paul had put it rather differently (Romans 5:7), knowing how hard it was to die: 'why, one will hardly die for a righteous man - though perhaps for a good man one will dare even to die.' And from our own time we have the example of St Maximilian Kolbe who offered himself at Auschwitz to take the place of a fellow Pole, married and with children, when the Nazis had chosen 40 victims to die of starvation in response to one prisoner who had escaped.

Actually Maximilian Kolbe's is an interesting case (I am indebted to Wikipedia for what follows). He was beatified by Pope Paul VI who named him a Confessor and gave him the unofficial title 'martyr of charity'. But this was not enough for Pope John Paul II who wanted to show that the Nazis' hatred of whole categories of humanity was inherently also a hatred of the Christian faith, and thus Kolbe's death equated to earlier examples of martyrdom suffered for the sake of religion.

Martyr comes from the Greek word meaning witness. A martyr is thus someone who witnesses, by his death, to the Christian faith. At the time Paul was writing persecution of the Jews had not yet become official imperial policy. This was to come later, under Nero and Domitian, and it is generally thought that Paul died by the sword (because he was a Roman citizen) under Nero towards the end of the sixties AD.

So is it possible to experience martyrdom without charity? One would hardly think so, from the examples given above. Yet, oddly enough, it is easier to conceive of this than it was to think of faith unaccompanied by charity. Thomas à Becket says as much in T S Eliot's play *Murder in the Cathedral* when he speaks of 'doing the right deed for the wrong reason'. The wrong reason is to seek temporal power, to 'bind king and bishop under [your] his heel'. And there are other wrong reasons that one can think of: there is, though one can hardly imagine it, an auto-eroticism about martyrdom, likely to be particularly prevalent when others are being martyred and a kind of ecstatic wish to share their fate embraces one. Then there is a desire to acquire a glorious name; and finally a longing to be with God in heaven before he decrees it. All these are examples of what Becket calls 'the greatest treason' and they are condemned by Paul because they are not done out of the greatest virtue, charity.

Martyrdom, in other words, is not something to be sought, though it may be desired, and even, by those willing to endure its pain, embraced with joy. This was so particularly in the early days of the Church, as a means of being reunited with God in heaven. Others have taken every step to avoid it; and this is often not cowardice, though it is natural to fear burning or the executioner's sword, but prudence, a virtue to be admired and not condemned. One such, who did not wish for martyrdom, but did not flinch from it when it was thrust upon him, was St Thomas More, who regarded silence as the best way of avoiding it. He had every reason to stay alive: a family, friends, a high reputation, literary skills. Arraigned, finally, in 1535 and accused of treason by denying the king's supremacy, he kept steadfastly silent, hoping that by this means he would not be convicted. But, as in Jesus' case, false witnesses were brought to say that he had spoken out against it, and it was only when he had been found guilty that he let himself go, saying that it was wrong for Henry to declare himself head of the Church of

England, a role that belonged to the Pope alone and could not be taken from him. He was sentenced to death, a fate he bore with equanimity, refusing all efforts to make him recant.

With this example we come to the end of this section of Paul's discourse on charity, in which he states that even the greatest acts of devotion or self-sacrifice are worthless unless accompanied by charity. And so we long to learn what this gift of charity is all about; and this we will learn in the next verses.

5. VERSES 4-5

Patient and kind

Few would disagree that these are qualities we need to
show in our dealings with others if we are to be thought
charitable. Paul is talking about this kind of charity,
charity governing our behaviour to others, rather than the
kind I have already discussed, the charity which we need
to show towards ourselves when we fall short of our
intentions. We know this because the whole chapter is on
this theme, our relation to our neighbour, and one of the
good things that has emerged from this virus infection is
that it has made us slightly more aware of others. Whereas
for instance, many of us in the past would walk with eyes
firmly down in case we should have to meet and
acknowledge our neighbours, now it is common, when
taking our daily exercise, to smile and actually greet those
whom we pass. Goodness knows whether this will persist
when the crisis is past, or whether we shall retreat to our
solitary state once more.

In a way this is an age which makes more demands on
our patience than most, and at least part of this can be put
down to technology. Whereas in the past some of us, at
least, might have opened up to our neighbour, now it is
common to find, even walking in the street and blind to
upcoming traffic, everyone with phones glued to their ears.
They do this even when paying for services, bus fares for
instance, or shopping, and often their conversations sound
as if they were of the most banal kind, simply telling their
partner they are on the train and will be home soon.

But another thing that strains our patience is being kept
on the phone ourselves, not knowing how long we will
have to wait, while a confident voice urges us to hang on
because the call is so important to them. Then, when we

finally get through, we are faced with a bewildering array of options, and whichever we choose, we have to make our needs known to a machine rather than to an individual person. It is no surprise if some of us put down our phones in disgust; or, if we finally succeed in talking to a live person, vent our anger. But we should remember that the person concerned is not responsible for the delay: they are simply doing their job; and if anyone deserves our anger, it is the one at the top of the chain, often earning millions, who has not bothered to install a satisfactory answering system.

I am not saying this is the only source of our irritation. But it plays a large part in it, and is a sign of the way society is speeding up and becoming more impersonal. Of course there is a good side to this. Young people, in particular, spend much more time talking to each other than they formerly did (though one should not forget online bullying, which has been known to drive those affected to suicide). But it is questionable how valuable this sort of interaction is, how superficial indeed, compared to that which allows one to see the other person's face, to take account of their moods, and to end with a gesture that shows how worthwhile the conversation was.

Was Jesus himself patient and kind? It is certainly easy enough to find instances where he was impatient: with his opponents, for instance (Luke 11:42, Matt 11:21), with the uncommitted (Matt 8:20), and even with Peter after he had first designated him head of the Church (Matt 16:22). On the other hand simply being with his disciples must have required a great deal of patience at times. He spent three years training them; yet until the end (Acts 1:6), they did not really understand what sort of Messiah he was, how he must suffer and rise again on the third day (Mark 9:31). He had constantly to face their ambition and their inner quarrelling (Mark 9:33) and, above all, though he gave up his position in heaven voluntarily, it must at times have galled him to adopt what Paul calls (Philippians 2:7) the form of a servant and stand silent in front of Pilate.

As regards his kindness, we are not often told of the personal feelings that accompanied his miracles; but several stand out. His pity is explicitly mentioned when he raised the widow's son (Luke 7:11), when he healed the leper (Mark 1:40), and when he fed the five thousand (Mark 6:34); and it is impossible to conceive that he was without compassion when he raised Jairus' daughter, and on the way healed the woman who had been suffering from a haemorrhage for twelve years. There is no greater charity than that of Jesus who laid down his life not simply for his friends, but for those who were yet to come, who were still ignorant of his name. So, yes, Jesus was both patient and kind, though these are not necessarily the first things one thinks about him. And I have always distrusted those who say 'what would Jesus do in these circumstances?' For it is all too easy to manipulate the answer so that it favours oneself. Whereas the thing to do is to consult one's own conscience, or to seek in prayer the guidance of the Holy Spirit.

Is it possible to be too kind? It depends, of course, how one interprets the word 'kindness'; but again, taking one's example from Jesus, one should not let kindness degenerate into softness. He may have saved the woman caught in adultery from her persecutors; but before letting her go he admonished her not to sin again. He was not afraid to talk of sin (Matt 15:18-20) or even to accompany his healing miracles with the injunction that the person healed should sin no more (John 5:14), though one suspects that in this instance he was pandering to the man's belief that sin was responsible for his paralysis. So giving in to people is not always the answer.

Patience and kindness start in the family. But, as Jesus says, this is not enough. Plenty of people love their families, but fail to extend that love to others. And even within the family gross situations take place which give the lie to the theory that families are the source of all love.

A telling statistic has been that during this time of lockdown reports of domestic abuse have enormously increased. It seems that some people are simply not suited to being close to others the whole time, which is why, to quote another statistic, divorce rates have a way of increasing after Christmas. Yet Paul gives excellent advice about how we should behave in families. 'Do not let the sun go down on your anger,' he says (Eph 4:26). In other places he tells husbands to love their wives as Christ loved the church (Eph 5:25). Admittedly he is less in tune with modern life when he tells wives always to be subject to their husbands (Eph 5:22), but he sounds surprisingly up to date when he tells fathers - and this applies to mothers too - after telling their children to obey their parents, not to provoke their children (Col 3:21) lest they should become discouraged. Family life, in short, depends on each individual recognising the other as a person in his or her own right, and this is sometimes forgotten, even in Christian families.

When we move to the outside world we come into contact with a great number of people to whom we are largely indifferent. Some, in time, become friends, and we have no difficulty relating to them and even, in certain circumstances, in putting their will before our own. But, as I say, there are a large number to whom we remain totally indifferent, and this is a situation that we should endeavour to put right. Often when we get to know such people better, we find that they are surprisingly interesting, and that they have something rewarding to give us. So what is it that prevents us giving the time of day to such people in the first place, exploring their needs, and trying to make friends of them?

Each of us has a built in need for reticence, to be ourselves, when we pass from closeness of the family, not, as I say, always the breeding ground of love it should be; and the English are notorious for their reserve, staying silent in railway carriages - thank God now for mobile phones which at least give the illusion that we are engaged in meaningful relationships - and positively frowning when anyone attempts to break into that silence. I do not know if other nations have the equivalent of the saying 'An Englishman's home is his castle,' but if so, it is a saying which should be disregarded. We only become Christian when we use every ounce of imagination, every resource we have, to create relationships with others. And this often exposes us to humiliation or rebuff; but even in these circumstances we should persevere. For God gave us these faculties not to hide them away (Matt 5: 15-16), but to make the fullest possible use of them, including towards those with whom we do not feel a natural affinity.

The fact that we do not do so and that we employ perhaps only half of what is available to us, can in part be put down to lack of imagination. We do not realise that each man is a brother to us, each woman a sister. We are content to treat as such those who are closest to us, colleagues at work, people with whom we have a natural affinity, friends and so on. But how many people does this actually comprise? What we fail to realise is that even those whom we casually brush up against, those with whom we have apparently nothing in common, deserve the same sort of treatment.

I am not suggesting that we become card-carrying Christians, that we go about proclaiming our allegiance, that we are constantly on the look-out for friends, and make ourselves bores or fools by repeatedly trying to initiate a conversation with complete strangers. But there are all sorts of people with whom we come into daily contact and with whom our relationship goes no further than a hurried hullo, followed by a desire to escape as quickly as possible to the next thing. Perhaps if we developed these relationships further, we would as I say, find them rewarding, for regardless of what they led to, they would at least yield the glow of satisfaction that accompanies each new action, each venture undertaken successfully. What I am arguing is that we should not keep part of ourselves hidden from others, even if this involves an effort to break the wall of silence with which we are comfortable, even if this sometimes exposes us to embarrassment or humiliation. There is no other way, perhaps, to be a complete Christian. Paul does not say as much; but then he was confronted with the same situation every day of his life. He had to broach conversation with complete strangers: otherwise he would never have got his gospel message across. Maybe he was a more intimate sort of person, who would have preferred to choose his own friends, or even to have been left alone in peace. Maybe he would have thought, if he had not been called, that this was enough, as many of us in fact do. We are content to make friends with people with whom we have something in common, and this applies particularly to those who have the same faith as us, but there are still others whom we regard as worthy of no further attention.

This is simply akin to the relationships we make within our families, which Christ says is not enough. And though there are other reasons for this, to be discussed later, the fact that it never enters our thoughts to express ourselves further is in part a failure of imagination.

But what of those whom we genuinely dislike, whom we have made an effort to know and with whom we are certain we shall never get on? I think it is prudent in such cases simply to retreat, to treat them politely, of course, but to realise that we are never going to succeed. It happens to us quite frequently with people with whom others have no difficulty at all. Indeed, if called upon to express an opinion, they would totally fail to understand how we feel. All one can say in such circumstances is that each of us is made in a different way. Person A gets on perfectly well with person B whereas person C finds B unacceptable. And I do not say that we should make a point of seeking out those whom, through some quirk of our own, we shall never get on with. I am not a fan of what, at the risk of giving offence, may be called the masochistic side of Christianity, that regards no action as worthwhile unless it brings pain or suffering in its wake.

There is a certain affinity here, however much humbler the scale, with martyrdom: one should not pursue it, although, if it is forced upon one, one has no alternative but to accept it.

Jealous and boastful

Jealousy, translated as envy in the King James version, and expressly forbidden by the ten commandments, is a singularly barren emotion. Envy itself is not to be wholly despised, since it can lead to emulation: the cricketer, for instance, envious of his rival who scores more runs than him, can strive to emulate his technique and so improve his batting. But as we find in the Old Testament it can also lead to murder (1 Kings 21) or adultery followed by murder (2 Samuel 11) and it is probably in this sense that the ten commandments refer to it. Jealousy, however, has nothing good to be said about it: it is a totally negative emotion, something which poisons the soul, and is not easily expunged once it is there.

It is often used in a sexual sense, and described by Iago, in Shakespeare's play *Othello*, as the 'green-eyed monster' which, once one is its victim, preys chiefly on the imagination and will not let one go (Iago, incidentally, is adept in feeding Othello's jealousy by the use of a single word, as when he alters (IV.1) Othello's 'lie with her' to 'lie on her'). But of course it need not refer solely to sex. One can be jealous of a neighbour's family love; of his ease in getting on with people; of his promotion; of his car. But, I repeat, jealousy of this kind is a totally negative emotion, it simply feeds on itself and leads to no remedial action on one's part.

In this sense it can be compared with other negative emotions which, however bad, do at least seem to have something positive about them. Hatred, for instance, also something which one feeds on, can provide a degree of satisfaction and create the illusion that one is alive. But jealousy can never do that. It is one of the most powerful emotions, but also the most destructive, that exists.

In what follows I am using it in perhaps a sense that Paul did not entirely intend, referring to occasions when we are jealous of another person's good qualities, in other words of his 'niceness.' It is surely this which prompts Cain's killing of Abel (Gen 4:8), for until this point we have learnt of no quarrel between them. His sacrifice has been refused whereas Abel's has been accepted. but there is no inherent difference in the sacrifices. Can it be, therefore, that Cain's is offered in the wrong spirit, that he is anticipating Christ's command (Matt 5:23-24) that before making our offering we should first be reconciled with our brother if we have anything against him.

Jealousy in this sense is a particularly ugly emotion, and it cannot be wholly banished from the spiritual life. For, particularly if one is after perfection oneself, it is common to see others who are more advanced along the spiritual ladder; and in this sense, I would guess, it is hard to avoid in the religious life where another's virtues are constantly in front of one's face. It is so unfair, one thinks, I go to Mass more often than he or she; I give more in the collection; I do my best to please everyone with whom I come into contact. Yet people appear to prefer the other person to me, they think more highly of him. What can I do about this? Well, there is one simple remedy, though it may not be to everyone's liking, may not, indeed, solve the problem of jealousy with which our imaginary person is inflicted. It is to reflect that everyone is loved in the same way by God; and that if one feels inferior to others, it is because one does not love him in the same way. The parable of the labourers in the vineyard (Matt 20:1) gives an excellent example of this. Those who have toiled all day are angry because they only receive the same reward as those who have only worked for one hour. But the householder responds, perfectly reasonably, that both have fulfilled the terms of the contract they accepted. One may not like the answer: indeed, the person whose case we are considering will almost certainly not. But it is the only answer he will be given. He must learn to accept that each person's good qualities are a gift only to himself; that he has no right to envy others and that he must strive, in his own way, to love God more.

Few of us are as openly boastful as President Trump, who claims never to have done anything that requires God's forgiveness. Most of us are content with some slight reference to our achievements, letting it drop that we have just published a book, received an OBE, or otherwise distinguished ourselves. One of the commonest ways of being boastful is name dropping. We let it be known that we have recently moved in grand company. This is all the more effective if we refer to the person concerned by his or her Christian name: eg "I was having dinner with Darcey last week" or "Grayson told me yesterday." This makes it plain that the speaker is on intimate terms with the celebrity concerned, leaves us to guess who it means, and implies that we would instantly know who was being referred to if only we moved in such distinguished company.

An innocent form of boasting is when we wish to share our joy with others. In each of the cases listed above, for instance - publication of a book or receiving a decoration - it may have come unexpectedly and we let out our joy as we would at the birth of a child. But not all boasting - and the examples I have just given can hardly be labelled boasting - can be as innocent. We are out to impress, and any way in which we can express our superiority is sufficient.

Jesus explicitly warns us against seeking to draw attention to ourselves for our good deeds (Matt 6: 2-6). He contrasts the way his followers should behave with that of hypocrites, saying that when they pray, they should go into an inner room and pray in secret; when they fast, they should not draw attention to themselves by their countenance, but anoint their face and wash their head, and generally look cheerful.

John of the Cross links this up to those embarked on the spiritual life by saying that, however delightful their experience of contemplation may be, they should realise that it is not the end of their spiritual journey, and risk losing sight of their destination if they seek to dwell in it for ever.

Boastfulness can be overt or something kept to oneself. Those who are always boasting of their achievements are soon found out. They risk becoming bores, and even if the tale they are telling is true, they are often not believed (anglers' tales have passed into proverbial use in this regard). Inner boastfulness is more subtle. It is natural to feel a sense of self-congratulation when one has done a good deed, and no one would seek to deny a spiritual person that reward. But the danger, as John of the Cross says of those who are seeking perfection by prayer, is if one thinks that that is all that is required of one, that this is one's good action for the day. Paul might well have added that the need for charity never stops, that we cannot be content with a single instance of it. It is something that is demanded of us the whole time, that should govern all our lives.

Open boasting is often a sign of insecurity, of seeking to reassure ourselves when we are not certain that reassurance from others will come our way. Reassurance, whether consciously or unconsciously, is one of the things we are most on the look-out for, and it frequently governs our conversations. This is why I say that, in certain stages of the spiritual life, when one is seeking to give rather than to receive, one often feels naked and afraid. The defences that we normally expect in our everyday encounters are gone. But we should not let this disturb us. Even if we feel that others do not recognise our worth, we should take comfort in the fact that God loves us, that he is aware of every single act we think or do, and that he forgives the boastfulness that comes over us when we think we have done well. This, in itself, should be sufficient reward.

Arrogant and rude

An arrogant person is one in whose company one scarcely feels one exists, so convinced is he of his own superiority, so reluctant to hear anything one wants to say. Even if he listens to us for a brief moment, even if whatever advice we have to give to him does not go in one ear and out of the other, it is forgotten as soon as we leave.

Hitler was such an individual. Apart from his more obvious acts of aggression, such as trying to annihilate the whole Jewish race and waging war whenever he found it possible, he rarely listened to his generals' advice, so convinced was he of his own military genius, which certainly served him well in the early days of his career. If he had heeded them, maybe the war would have taken a different course, or at least not gone on for so long. And the same characteristic can be found in many contemporary leaders, who wage war supposedly on their nations' behalf, and often reward themselves with grandiose palaces at the end of the day.

The opposite of arrogance is meekness, a quality which we are not disposed to think much of nowadays. 'Gentle Jesus, meek and mild' is the first line of one of Charles Wesley's hymns, but we would be inclined to repudiate the image, and think of him as a much stronger character. The way we think of meekness is on a par with the image of 'spiritual childhood', an expression often attributed to St Thérèse of Lisieux, but which she in fact never used. But it is a virtue commended by Jesus in the beatitudes, and it consists of knowing one's place in society, and of even being prepared to sacrifice one's own principles if that seems the best thing to do, if it is the only way to obtain something resembling peace. As such it is a virtue much needed in the present world and perhaps there would be fewer wars if all leaders of nations were to embrace it, wars which are often the result of wounded pride.

Something has already been said of rudeness. It is often the result of an injury suffered on one occasion and the blow to one's pride being carried over to the next. The example I gave was of being kept waiting for what seems like hours on the telephone, finally getting through and taking out one's resentment on the unfortunate who happens to answer the call. But rudeness is observable at all levels of the way we live. When we have a minor car accident, for instance, it is always the other person's fault, never our own.

Rudeness is unfortunately endemic in our society, and is probably linked to the way life has speeded up in the last few years, and our demand for instant answers to our questions and doubts. But it is certainly undesirable, leads to other faults, and society would function much better if it was eliminated.

Paul's list of virtues to be cultivated and faults to be eschewed applies both to Christians and non-Christians, and is widely recognised as something that must be observed if we wish society to run smoothly. But the difference between the two groups is that it is mandatory in the case of the former. We simply cannot choose when to be charitable, how much of our energy should be devoted to it, or whether we should treat it as an ideal put there to inspire us, but decidedly out of our reach. There is nothing optional about it.

This is why I say that the failure of most Christians to embrace perfection, or even to embark on the path that leads towards it, is as much as anything due to a lack of imagination. Other things, of course, come into it. It is a hard life, and makes great demands upon one. It is hardly surprising if many Christians shy away from it, and are content with merely fulfilling the easy part of their Christian duties and thinking that this is enough. But this is not the life St Paul, and certainly not Jesus, expected us to live. In their minds charity had to be something continuous, something which we recognised as our duty, and not something to be taken up simply when we felt like it.

This was widely recognised by the saints of old, and led to the detailed analysis of prayer undertaken by such acknowledged experts as Saints Teresa and John of the Cross. But their attention was almost entirely focused on others who like themselves lived in religious institutions.

But now attention has switched to the world outside, to those not called to the religious life; and so far there has been no organised way expressed for them to reach perfection, or indeed widespread recognition of the need for them to do so. So progress has to proceed on two fronts. On the one hand there is the need to persuade the laity that perfection is within their grasp, that it is an ideal to be pursued; and secondly the means by which it can be achieved should receive widespread recognition. No better example to help us on our way can be found than the text we have been examining.

6. VERSES 5-8

Does not insist on its own way

It is a curious fact that in many situations we seek to have the last word, even if the argument or whatever it was has been long settled, when having this last word will not reopen it, but is just something without which we feel that life would not be complete. It is easy to put this down to immaturity, to the fact that in our childhood we have never learnt to give in. But it may also be a sign of something which has already been dealt with in these pages: the wish to dominate.

On the face of it discussions we have even with our close partners take place on equal terms. We neither seek to give in too much nor to assert ourselves. In effect however - and this applies not only to intimate discussions, but to a much wider range of topics - two things are underway. On the one hand there is the subject of conversation, and this may be no more than an arrangement to meet at a certain place or time, or a decision as to whose turn it is pick up the children from school today. But it may well be that something extra is going on. Each is looking for a way of imposing his will on the other; and this is because in conversation we are primarily looking for reassurance.

Sometimes the conversation will come after one has lost this reassurance for the moment. Something may have happened to disturb one. One may have been bruised in one way or another. What more natural then that one should look to the next person to restore this reassurance? Ideally in the family there should be no need for this. One should have built up sufficient trust in one's partner to know that whatever one tells them their love will not cease. But unfortunately this is not always the case. Nasty quarrels can build up which a single word of reconciliation could solve. But neither of them is willing to give in at this point. And so the quarrel festers and is added to all the things which the couple do not have in common, but which may have drawn them together in the first place, or at least may have been until then a source of amusement. Sometimes the situation becomes so bad that the children suffer; and then divorce or separation may be the answer. But looking back one can see many points at which the discord could have been solved. If only one partner had been willing to give up their will for an instant to realise that saving the marriage was far more important than any satisfaction of the ego which a temporary victory would bring. But no: one is too attached to one's pride, too ready not to let any occasion go by which it may be upheld. And so divorce follows, which is a messy expensive business, and everybody, including the children, suffers.

During our time we have become acutely aware of the issue of domestic violence and many homes have sprung up in which women can take refuge from an abusive partner. But it is important to realise that women are not the only ones who suffer in these situations. Men too can have their spirit broken and they may be less ready to admit to it, because somehow a henpecked husband is a greater source of amusement than a damaged wife. One of the great achievements of our time has been to recognise that women have the same rights as men, that they are equally capable of reaching decisions and solving problems. But by the same token it must be recognised that they are also capable of being as dominant as men; and both sexes need protection when this arises.

Irritable and resentful

These two things have certain features in common and can be dealt with under one heading. They are also similar to other faults which have already been discussed. Resentment, like jealousy, is a negative emotion. That is to say, it is often convenient to let it continue to fester away rather than to attempt to do something about it.

Where would we be without the 'they' or 'them' whom it is so convenient to blame in such circumstances? Often we do not even specify who 'they' are: it is more useful to lump them under one heading, to see them as people in charge who should not have let this happen to us, who should have acted sooner. Probably we mean by this the politicians who govern our country, and it must be admitted that they have done a lot to deserve this obloquy.

Probably there has never been a time when politicians were more distrusted than today, and this is due to the lies they tell. Of course politicians have always told lies: Churchill's refusal to accept anything less than final victory, for instance, may have saved us during the war; but though never concealing from the British people the dangers that faced them, he was choosy when it came to telling the whole truth, particularly about incidents which went badly wrong. Nowadays, however, we almost take it for granted, sometimes unfairly, that politicians will do almost anything to gain or stay in office. An easy example from nowadays is the constant repetition that everything possible was done at the start of the pandemic to protect care homes, when everyone knows that this was not true, and that patients were released from hospital without testing. Another that winning the referendum would immediately make £350,000,000 a week available for the NHS.

Sometimes, particularly under dictatorships, these lies are carried to extremes, a prime example being North Korea where the people are expected to believe everything their leader tells them, when it is plain that many of them are suffering from undernourishment or even starvation. But even in so-called democracies the lies are so blatant that they take the form of cynicism rather than an outright wish to deceive. Everybody knows, for instance, that the Russians were ultimately responsible for the destruction of Malaysia Airlines flight 17, the plane shot down over Ukraine, and that there was indisputable proof of this. But the Russians continue to deny it, and what turns this into cynicism is that they know that the world knows it to be untrue. In other words they do not expect to be believed. Is it surprising, then, that when major powers behave in this way, it rubs off on all governments and they become universally distrusted?

And then there is conspiracy theory. Some of the doubts that people raise appear perfectly reasonable, and it is natural to hold them. It is hard, for instance, to believe that Lee Harvey Oswald could have fired off three shots so quickly, on his own, and so there must have been another assailant involved. But when the House of Representatives select committee has thoroughly looked into the matter and come to the opposite conclusion, it then becomes conspiracy theory to believe that the contrary is true and that 'they' have something to conceal which they are not revealing to us.

Conspiracy theories occur all the time: over, for instance, the suicide of David Kelly, accused of exaggerating the threat from Saddam Hussein; over the origins of the coronavirus; over UFO's (though this is largely discredited now); over vaccination. The most egregious I have ever heard - and it was uttered in my presence - was that the attack on the Twin Towers was a vast CIA plot to discredit the Muslim community. We can see through some of these and dismiss them as fanciful; but the question has to be asked: would they have arisen had not governments lied to us in the past and would continue to lie to us in the future?

It seems impossible in our present society to believe that things are the result of natural phenomena or can be classed as accidents. Scaffolding does collapse - all right, this may be somebody's fault, but it can also be due to wind. Babies do die in hospital, floods and forest fires do occur, aeroplanes do sometimes drop from the sky. It is natural to look for causes for such incidents, and even to criminally prosecute those responsible. But sometimes, even after the most exhaustive enquiries, it is found that no one is to blame. Some people put such resentment as is left into founding scholarships in the memory of their dead relative, or in trying to enact laws which will prevent the repetition of such disasters. But for many it is an excuse for holding on to the belief that they have always held, that life, and particularly the authorities, are unfair; and sometimes they go on holding this belief for as long as they are alive, and it comforts them, and gives them something to live for.

It is hardly surprising that resentment and irritability are closely linked. For if one is perpetually convinced that one is being misled, then it is likely that one will feel perpetually annoyed about it; and, as I say, some people cling to this sense of annoyance because without it they would have nothing to live for. Irritability differs from anger in that it is a perpetual state, which may at any moment break into anger, but will remain even after the outburst. We have seen already what sort of harm it may do in the family, and even with colleagues at work. But they are not the only ones to suffer. The person who suffers this irritability will suffer himself as more and more people will avoid him, and he gets a reputation for thoroughly bad temper. This, in turn, will probably add to his sense of resentment. 'Nobody likes me. I am under some sort of cloud. They've got it in for me specially.' And unless he is careful that will cloud his whole life.

It also differs in that a sudden burst of anger can sometimes be beneficial. It clears the air, and after it one may be able to make up and regain one's equanimity. But irritability is never good, since it is based on a permanent sense of grievance.

Does not rejoice at wrong

It is hard to conceive of anyone rejoicing in another's sin, though it might remind one of one's own imperfections, and thus be a source of comfort or relief. One remembers Iago's words about Cassio (*Othello V.i*)

He hath a daily beauty in his life

That makes me ugly.

It is thus possible to feel other people's goodness as a reproach, and certainly possible to rejoice in their misfortunes. The Germans even have a word for it, *schadenfreude*, though there is no single word equivalent for it in English. We are all capable of taking pleasure in another's fall, particularly one who, we feel, has had more than his fair share of luck.

The British have a peculiar attitude towards those whom they revere. Once past a certain age, for instance, it is almost impossible to do any wrong. One becomes a grand old man or woman, and every word one says is listened to with attention. I would cite David Attenborough or Judi Dench here, except that it would suggest that they did not deserve such praise, that there was something murky in their past that had been conveniently overlooked. What is it that leads to such a reaction? Is it that they have lived so long, and this is a miracle in itself? Or is it that, having reached such an old age, we imbue them with every sort of wisdom that we associate with the old?

We also in this country - and I dare say this applies to other nations as well - have a curiously ambivalent attitude towards wealth and celebrity. On the one hand we admire such people and cannot have enough of them, particularly if they have left school at sixteen, worked for two years as a barrow boy, and come up with some marvellous invention which they have had to develop in their own back yard. It is the same with celebrities. We may not know what they are famous for, but they regularly appear on television, have their own chat shows, and the Queen may even have honoured them with an award. The *Sunday Times* regularly publishes its list of the wealthiest people in the country. Presumably it would not do this if it did not know that it was feeding into this mixture of awe and envy (inherited wealth by the way, does not produce the same reaction). We know we could never emulate such people, but that does not stop us regarding them with a certain tortuous admiration.

Then it all comes crashing down. They make some inadvertent remark which can loosely be construed as racist, or they are found in adultery with another man's wife. Suddenly nothing can be too bad for them. We revel in each subsequent discovery of the flaws in their moral character. It is probable that they can never recover the reverence they once held. At best they will be tolerated; some shadow will always hang over them.

I must admit that I am guilty of the same fault. Though I do not exactly delight in their fall, I like reading about the sexual misdemeanours of the great: I suppose it is something to do with the fact that they were never so good after all, that the media have built them up to an unrealistic extent, and it turns out that they were no different from the rest of us, with the same desires and vices. It must be acknowledged that the media do have a lot to do with this. The tabloids, in particular, surround people with adulation, and are the first to tear into them when something goes wrong. Day after day they fill the headlines, even if there is nothing more to discover about them, and in this way the   popular media are guilty of pandering to our worse instincts.

Probably many of us would not acknowledge the delight we take in such reversals to be a fault, and would not feel guilty about it. But if it is not exactly St Paul's 'does not rejoice at wrong' it comes near it. The trouble is that we have become so accustomed to this way of life that it is not considered an evil habit. Christian theology tells us that we should refrain from evil thoughts, even if they do not lead to evil deeds. But who can resist a good scandal? And the advice that the churches give here can seem to have something prissy about it.

To counter this Paul says that we should rejoice in the right. but some of us are not capable of doing even this. Gore Vidal, the American novelist, famously said 'Whenever a friend succeeds, some little something in me dies.' He is probably speaking here of other novelists, but we have seen how his applies in the spiritual life too. It is perfectly possible to envy those who seem more charitable than oneself. And the only remedy is to concentrate on one's own life, on own's own efforts to be charitable. How anyone else advances in the spiritual life is none of one's business; and if one can acquire this gift, if one is capable of recognising good in others and being genuinely grateful for it, one is, as Jesus told the scribe who asked him which was the greatest of the commandments (Mark 12:34), not far from the kingdom of heaven.

Paul ends this part of his encomium on charity with a fine rhetorical flourish, rightly translated in the version I am using as 'Love bears all things, believes all things, hopes all things, endures all thing.' But he cannot mean this without some further explanation. We have seen, for instance, how he is not exactly complimentary about the Athenians who did indeed believe all things. They even had a statue dedicated to an unknown god. His task was to teach the one true gospel of Christ, and he would certainly not have wanted his listeners to believe all things, or even to hope all things. He probably meant that they should accept what he was teaching them, in other words believe without reservation the one true gospel and set all their hopes on the fact that they had been redeemed, called to a new life, and that Christ would come again in majesty to judge the world.

Conscious of these possible confusions, the Jerusalem Bible, at least in its unrevised form which is the one I possess, has as its version 'it is always ready to excuse, to trust, to hope, and to endure whatever comes,' which does not have the same rhythm and may not be exactly what Paul had in mind. Generally speaking, I am not in favour of translations departing from the literal sense and giving their own interpretations. Else where is it to end? The Bible is full of things that either contradict each other or at least require some explanation. But in this case the Jerusalem version is conscious that the text as it stands leads to uncertainties. It has made a genuine effort to make plain its meaning and for this one should be grateful.

7. VERSES 8-13

The first part of St Paul's paean in praise of charity has been devoted to asserting its place at the very heart of Christianity, without which we are nothing, and describing what we must do in order to be described as charitable. The second part states its superiority to all other virtues, including those always prized by the Church, faith and hope, as the only one that will last when we finally take our place in heaven.

This was nothing original he had to say. The last commandment Jesus had given to his disciples (John 15:12) had been that they should love one another, as he himself had loved them. This justifies our placing love, or charity, as our supreme task on earth, something that the Church has not always recognised, or perhaps more truly misinterpreted, as an excuse for putting people to death in order to save their souls. Paul had not been present when Jesus spoke the words above, and the gospels had not yet been written when he wrote to the Corinthians. It is possible that he had heard Jesus' words from others; but what is much more likely is that, in the course of his remedial sojourn in Arabia, he had come to realise this truth. It did not stop him preaching, of course. He is probably the greatest preacher the Church has ever known, and his whole life was devoted to trying to turn away first the Jews, and then anyone who would listen to him, from their incomplete notion of God, or the false deities they had worshipped in the past, to the one true God manifested in Jesus Christ. But even after telling all this to the Corinthians, and reprimanding them for their faults, it is this to which he returns: charity is the supreme virtue, and if they do nothing else, they must strive to emulate Jesus in their love.

Another who knew of the supremacy of love was John the evangelist. He had been present at the Last Supper, and must therefore have heard Jesus' last commandment, and he testifies to its importance in his first letter, which is almost on a par with what Paul has to say:

Beloved, let us love one another; for love is of God, and he who loves is born of God and knows God...No man has ever seen God; if we love one another, God abides in us and his love is perfected in us. (1 John 4:7-12)

He was the most perceptive of Jesus' disciples, and it is to the words of both that we must return if we would seek to know the essentials of our faith.

Paul here cites prophecies, tongues and knowledge as the three things destined eventually to pass away. We have seen his attitude towards knowledge, and no more needs to be said on that subject. But the other two require further discussion, starting with prophecy.

As we have seen, prophets in the Old Testament were primarily people who recalled Israel to their first task of loving and serving God who had brought them out of Egypt. The Jews were a volatile people who regularly forgot this commandment and, largely under the influence of their monarchs - we are told (1 Samuel 8) that God was very reluctant to grant them kings - fell into the habit of worshipping idols. Or, when disaster struck - and the worst disaster of all was when they were conquered and transported, first to Assyria, and later to Babylon - they lost hope; and it was up to the prophets to convince them that it was through their own fault that they had lost God's favour, and that they must do everything in their power to regain it.

The New Testament writers were very anxious to show that all that had happened since, and particularly the coming of Jesus, had been foretold by the Jewish writers who were thus prophets in the modern sense of the word, people who could foretell the future as well as recall Israel to its primary task of loving God. We actually have this gift shown in the Old Testament long before Jesus came on the scene. In Numbers, for instance, 24:17, Balaam, commanded by his king to curse Israel, said on the contrary

A star shall come forth out of Jacob,
    and a sceptre shall rise out of Israel;
It shall crush the forehead of Moab,
    and break down all the sons of Sheth.

The most famous of all the prophecies concerning Jesus occur in Isaiah 53, and are repeated in the readings at Passion-time:

He was despised and rejected by men:
    a man of sorrows, and acquainted with grief;
and as one from whom men hide their faces
    he was despised, and we esteemed him not.

Surely he has borne our griefs
    and carried our sorrows;
yet we esteemed him stricken,
    smitten by God, and afflicted.
But he was wounded for our transgressions,
    he was bruised for our iniquities.

It was natural that these words should be applied to Christ; and indeed it is possible that Isaiah, writing under the influence of the Holy Spirit, was indeed referring to a mystery which he could not fully understand.

In the gospels these attempts to make the present fit the past abound. Matthew, for instance, in 2:6, has the wise men come to see the infant Jesus refer to the verses in Micah 5:2, predicting that Bethlehem shall be his birthplace: and it was natural for Jesus himself (Matt 11:10) to refer to Malachi 3:1 when speaking of John the Baptist:

Behold, I send my messenger before thy face,
    who shall prepare thy way before thee.

Everything that happened during Jesus' life could thus be linked to what had been foretold in the Jewish Bible. Sometimes the connections strike one as very far-fetched. Matthew, for instance (27:9-10) speaking of Judas' attempt to return the money which he had just received for the betrayal of Jesus, refers one to Jeremiah. But when one looks up the quotation from Jeremiah (32: 6-15) one finds only the vaguest similarity between the two events.

Prophets in the modern sense of the word were not lacking in St Paul's time. Thus we read in Acts 11:28 of a disciple called Agabus who foretold that there would be a great famine over all the world; and just to prove that his words were true, we are further told that this took place in the days of the Emperor Claudius. But this is not the sense in which Paul commonly uses the word. To him it is much more akin to the way in which it was used in the Old Testament, of one with a special insight who had been commissioned by God to convey a message to his people. Thus in Acts 13:1 several are named prophets though they are also called teachers. By this token Paul certainly had the right to be called a prophet, though he preferred the term apostle (1 Cor 15:8-9), one born out of his time.

In 1 Corinthians 12:28 Paul labels prophets immediately after apostles in importance. He also begs the Corinthians (1 14:5) to be prophets themselves in order to edify the whole church of Christ. It seems here that he was asking them to do no more than be powerful preachers instead of being wrapped up in their own particular concerns and squabbles. He is also contrasting them with those speaking in tongues, of which more will be said in a minute, for in that way they will be of far greater use to the Church. It seems, therefore, that Paul is using the term in two ways, one of which is to signify a person who has a special message, who has been commissioned by God to enlighten the Church; and one, not necessarily inspired by God in a special way, but carrying the message of the gospel, and passing it on to others.

When we come to speaking in tongues, we must distinguish what happened to the disciples at Pentecost from the way Paul speaks of the phenomenon, which is also the way in which it occurs today in certain branches of the Christian faith. Pentecost was a genuine miracle: the assembled crowd all heard the apostles speak in their own languages, and they were fully able to understand them. This is called xenolalia as opposed to glossolalia, which is the phenomenon to which Paul refers and of which he was also a practitioner (1 Cor 14:18). But he also draws attention to what is the chief drawback of this gift, namely that it is not understood by all, and that it therefore requires an interpreter (1 Cor 12:10).

Glossolalia is the ecstatic speech by which worshippers convey their praise of God. It is quite unlike any other form of speech, and occurs at the height of prayer. It is rightly regarded as a gift of the Holy Spirit, is not as common as it once was, and may even be accompanied by acts bordering on the eccentric (such variations as the Toronto blessing have not helped its cause). Paul is therefore right in regarding it with a certain degree of scepticism. One could hardly deny that it was a gift of the Holy Spirit, and he lists it, with interpreters, at the end of chapter 13, as one of the gifts which together make up Christ's body. But it does require an interpreter (14:5), who has himself to learn the language, and may in any case diffuse the message once he has put it into plain speech; and surely it is better to speak plainly than in a language that no one can understand.

Paul spends no less than 19 verses on this subject, which makes one think that some of the Corinthians were so taken up with this phenomenon that they neglected the other, and essential, parts of the faith. In the course of these 19 verses he gives many illustrations:

> If even lifeless instruments, such as the flute or the harp, do not give distinct notes, how will any one know what is played? (verse 7)

> If I pray in a tongue, my spirit prays, but my mind is unfruitful (14)

> In church I would rather speak five words with my mind, in order to instruct others, than ten thousand words in a tongue (19)

It is plain that at least as far as the Corinthians were concerned he would rather have done without it altogether.

It is a different matter with false prophets. Paul was constantly on the look-out for these. He mentions them in 2 Cor 11:13, again in verse 26, in Galatians 2:4…In this he is only echoing the words of Jesus who had said (Mark 13:22): 'False Christs and false prophets will arise and show signs and wonders to lead astray, if possible, the elect'. This was a real danger. Later the word heresy was used to describe such false prophets, and the Church had a hard time distinguishing false from true. Sometimes the heretics could be denounced or persecuted with extreme violence. Compared to these, therefore, those claiming to speak in tongues because it was fashionable could be dismissed as mere babblers. They were a nuisance, but they were not capable of leading the flock astray as were the false prophets.

Paul is plain, therefore, in stating (13:8) that these three things, knowledge, prophecies and tongues, will pass once we are granted the full sight of God in heaven. And the same might have been said of all those whom he has listed in an earlier chapter who help to build up the kingdom of God on earth: teachers, workers of miracles, healers, helpers, administrators (12:27). For the Church of God is a peculiar thing: it has always had one eye on heaven even while dealing with the situation on earth. Some consider that it can never be described as anything but perfect since it represents the Body of Christ. But others take a more realistic view, regarding it as far from perfect as we have seen from recent events; and the second eucharistic prayer, the one most frequently used for weekday Masses, asks that it may be 'perfected in charity' - notice the wording - something which it would hardly do if it were perfect already.

Over the years we have seen how the bidding prayers have evolved. I can't remember whether they existed when I first became a Catholic in 1958. Almost certainly not. The Second Vatican Council called for the church to be more involved in the affairs of the world. This was slow to catch on, and is not even now complete; and the bidding prayers are an example of this. Thirty or forty years ago they were almost exclusively for the good of the church, and for us, its members, that we might grow in faith and holiness. But now it is rare to find a church which does not include at least one reference to what is going on in the world.

This is most obvious in the daily Masses offered up at the present moment on the internet in which a prayer for the victims of the coronavirus, for those who tend to them, for governments which have to make tough decisions over how far to go in releasing people from total lockdown, and for the scientists who work for a vaccine, is commonly expressed. But often other prayers are included, from a concern about riots in America to a prayer for human rights in a country such as Iran. In fact often in my own church, when the virus is no longer with us, I learn first of an aeroplane disaster or a hospital fire through the bidding prayers before I have seen or heard about it on the news. And this is as it should be. The Church has to be involved in the affairs of the world. Charity compels it to be so, whether or not its other main concern, the spreading of faith, is concerned.

So in a sense Paul's hymn to charity is just as relevant today as it was in the time it was written. And what he says about its superiority to all other virtues is also relevant. For, returning to the chapter in Corinthians, faith and hope will have no place when we are finally reunited with God after death. We shall have no need of faith when we can see God face to face; and likewise the summit of our hopes has ben fully reached once we are reunited with him in heaven. The only thing hidden from our sight will be the date of Christ's second coming; but we shall be assured of our own personal salvation even if there still remain gaps in our understanding.

What follows in Corinthians seems at first sight disconnected from the past or from what is to come. From here Paul is apparently talking about something completely new. He is mentioning his childhood, when he spoke and thought as a child, and how he was forced to put aside childish ways when he became an adult. But what on earth has this got to do with charity, and his claim that it is the first of all virtues? A moment's reflection will show that it is closely linked to the conclusion of his message. For just as Paul had to grow up and put away childish things, so the Church will learn that what is required on earth, namely faith and hope, will pass away at its final consummation. There will be no more need of them there. For what is the point of faith when you can see God face to face? And what is left to hope for when the zenith of one's hopes has been reached? The only thing that will remain is love: for as St John said later (1 John 4:16) God *is* love, and we shall be joined in heaven to the eternal love that flows between the three members of the Trinity.

The rest of the chapter adds nothing new. It says that our knowledge here on earth is like that of a man who sees only dimly through a mirror - and does he have in mind here Plato's image of our earthly life being spent in a cave in which we can see only shadows of the real world passing on behind us? And he adds that, just as he hopes for perfect knowledge when this life is past, so he too will be fully understood then. This too is important to him, as it is with all of us, for we cannot know ourselves as we truly are until we see ourselves with the sight of God.

8. THE NEED FOR SANCTITY

I said earlier that in a sense Paul was teaching us nothing new. For we all know, consciously or unconsciously, that it is not our faith which guarantees us a place in heaven, but what we make of it. There is plenty in the New Testament to remind us of the fact. I recall, for instance the parable (Luke 16:19) of Dives and Lazarus. It was not his riches - we are told nothing of his faith, which would have been that of an orthodox Jew - that condemned Dives to hell. It was the fact that he did nothing about the poor man sitting at his gate, whose sores even the dogs licked - for surely this is an image of compassion, rather than something that further added to his agony. And when Dives begs that Lazarus may be sent to his brothers to warn them of their coming dangers, he is firmly told that they have Moses and the prophets whom they should heed. It was the same, in fact, under the Jewish religion as it is in the Christian. We have to regard those whom we meet with compassion, we have to show them charity: otherwise the faith which we profess is so much emptiness.

It may be that Dives, when he went out, simply did not notice Lazarus. He had long been accustomed to seeing him sitting in the same place so that the beggar no longer made any impact on his senses. And it is the same with us in much that should claim our attention on this earth. It is not that we are deliberately unkind. On the contrary, we probably make a resolution every time we attend Mass that from now on we will attempt to live a little more closely as Jesus intended us to. But we do not notice the things that require our attention. We take up charity, if at all, sporadically, as the need arises. But it is something of which we be constantly aware, something which we need to practise the whole time.

I also cited Thérèse of Lisieux who said how contrary to natural instincts was the service of God. Of course much of what we do runs contrary to our natural instincts. The whole of education - by which I mean not just formal education, but all that we learn in the course of our lives - teaches us that living according to our natural instincts is a recipe for disaster. William Golding's *The Lord of the Flies* shows how this works in adolescent life; but I am sure that few of us would put any restraint upon our sexual desires unless we were taught to do so.

This raises the question of the word 'natural' which can be held to mean different things under different circumstances. The Catholic Church, for instance, until quite recently held that it was not natural to seek a relationship with a member of the same sex. Heterosexuality was the norm: homosexuality, even when it did not lead to action, the sign of a dangerous and perverted instinct. Even now various branches of the Christian church hold on to this view, and put in place remedies for this trait which for good or bad is inbred in us (I say for good or bad because unfortunately in the Catholic church there is no real answer to this problem. Homosexuals are condemned to live a life of total chastity: even the remedy most of us adopt when we feel we have done something wrong, namely to confess it to a priest, is invalid without a firm wish not to act in the same way again: and this is difficult for a homosexual who sees nothing wrong with his behaviour. It may be that this too is a consequence of how he has been treated in the past. Had he been told that the instinct to which he had been born did not run contrary to nature, he might have been willing to forgo the sexual activity which goes with it).

In a similar way what we consider 'natural' depends a lot on the stage we have reached and our general circumstance. Paul himself acknowledges this when he says that as a child it was natural for him to speak as a child and to think as a child, but that later came greater reflectiveness. We might consider this as it applies to our own behaviour. When we first become Christians, or at any rate become aware of what is required of us as Christians, a lot of things are off limits. For a long time confession was much more concerned with this: it dealt almost exclusively with the ways in which we had broken the Christian law. Now, fortunately, we realise that we are as much guilty for our failures as for the things we have done. The Mass begins with a prayer for pardon for 'the things I have done and the things I have failed to do'; and I personally believe that there should be yet more stress on the latter, that there is too much emphasis on Christianity as a religion of prohibitions rather than as one of opportunities.

If we turn to those who are generally regarded as the experts in the spiritual life, Saints Teresa and John of the Cross, we learn that it was wholly natural for those they were instructing to at least aim for perfection through the practice of prayer, and sometimes to achieve their ends. But something seems to have gone out of our religion since then. I have earlier said that this was because nothing had come to replace the discipline of prayer which the Spanish saints prescribed for their adherents. Since then the importance of the laity has been or is being recognised - it was only in 1867 that Talbot said 'What is the province of the laity? To hunt, to shoot, to entertain' - and while this was extreme even for its time, too often the laity's role has been seen as a passive one, merely to follow, to absorb, to obey.

The Second Vatican Council, however, said in *Lumen Gentium* that it was the role of all, laity as well as clerics, to seek holiness, in other words to work with as much dedication as the devotees of Teresa and John of the Cross to reach perfection. But there is a curious gap in lay theology as to how this is to be achieved. I also said that much closer attention should be paid to Thérèse of Lisieux as the model which we should follow.

True, she is widely accepted as a major saint of the Catholic church; and though many are put off by her prose style, many more are devoted to her notion of spiritual childhood, an expression, incidentally, which she never used. But much more important are the terms she used to define her spirituality: this is expressed as 'direct, short, and totally new'. If we consider only the last of these terms, it is plain that we have no option but to consider her as a revolutionary. Though maybe not fully conscious of it, she was turning over the wisdom which had been adopted at least since the time when Dionysus the Areopagite promulgated the idea of direct contact, through prayer, with God in this life. Her direct, short and totally new way was at odds with that of her Carmelite predecessors - whom, incidentally, she greatly revered - in that it advocated a spirituality based primarily on action.

Somehow 'the little way' sounds a bit infantile. Yes, if one is condemned to stay at home and has nothing better to do, it is entirely natural to offer up one's mundane tasks, be it washing up, cleaning the house, or even bringing up one's children to the glory of God, and to do these acts in the best possible way. It has been seen, in other words, primarily as its name suggests, as a way to pursue holiness meant chiefly for the stay-at-homes, those not much involved in worldly affairs; whereas its true nature is that it is applicable to all, whether it be a humble housewife, house-husband or the leader of a great nation. For it teaches us that we all have sanctity within our grasp, something which we must first realise and then pursue. It is thoroughly Pauline, in that is recognises charity as the greatest of Christian virtues, and considers all else dross if we do not possess it.

But does it work? Here one must turn to the first of the adjectives she gave it. It is 'direct', which means that it works quickly, without any palaver at all. And we should also consider the second adjective she gave it. It is 'short' (though we have no reason to infer that it is shorter than the model laid down by the Spanish saints; it is all a matter of the intensity with which one pursues it). But the combination of these three adjectives seems to me to convey that it is ideally suited to the lay life. The average lay person finds prayer hard and is often disinclined to persevere with it. There are so many different methods. And doubts arise: have I chosen the right one, nothing seems to happen. Have I spent the requisite time, is there another way I could get through more effectively to God? But with charity there can be no room for doubt. Either one has performed a charitable action or not. True, there may be cause for dissatisfaction. But at least one's action belongs in the main world. It is easy enough to see whether the intention to perform a charitable deed has been carried out or not.

This brings us back to the word 'natural'. What we can infer came naturally to Paul at this stage of his life, a total immersion in charity, may be far from natural to the average Christian. He or she is determined to obey the laws of the Church. They come to Mass regularly, say their prayers, try to put on a good face to the people they meet, and so on. But somehow it does not seem to occur to them that they could go further than this. I wrote earlier that the failure to aim for sanctity was in part a failure of imagination. Saints are for others. We learn about them, we admire them, we pray to them. But the idea that one could aim at sanctity for oneself passes the imagination.

Of course it is not simply a question of imagination. Even if the idea enters one's mind, there is still the discipline involved. It is not, in short, merely the wish to become a saint that transforms one. Before this there must be much effort, much willingness to endure hardship, and there will be many setbacks. But it is within everyone's capacity at least to try. And Thérèse has given us the requisite method.

So what does it take to advance on the way to perfection? I would say that the main requirement is extroversion. It means being constantly on the alert, with all one's senses focused on the outside world. This seems to run counter to what many have said of the spiritual life, that it requires a period of introversion in order to develop the faculties by which God can become known to the soul. But this advice was given when prayer was still seen as the main method of spiritual progress. When all is centred on prayer, it is natural that a period of quiet, or introversion, should be needed in order for the development of the faculty by which God communicates with us. For this does not solely depend on the senses. It is natural to suppose that God in prayer is speaking to us. It takes quite a lot of courage to face the fact that we are, as it were, alone in prayer: that is to say that God is certainly listening, but that the thoughts that arise are our own, much influenced, no doubt, by Church teaching and by what we think God expects of us, but no different in quality from the thoughts that arise at different times, no more a sign of God being significantly there than those.

It is perfectly true that a special faculty is required if we are to have direct communication with God, and this normally involves a period of introversion. Teresa, for instance, spends a chapter on this (*Interior Castle IV.iii)* and Ruth Burrows says that a bridge towards what we normally regard as contemplation is necessary in order that we should not be too disturbed by it. But what if we were to say that, instead of God preparing himself for us, requiring, in other words, a period of quiet by which he can build up this faculty of listening to him, we regard it as the other way? Yes, it does not come naturally. Time is needed before we are sufficiently ready to confront God directly, to receive his word in our souls; but what if the work is done on our part? We could consider, in other words, that instead of God creating this facility and requiring time to do so, it is we ourselves, through charity, who open ourselves up to him and thus become capable both of speaking to him and receiving his message? In this way the need for cessation from activity is past and we can safely continue with our charitable efforts based on the outside world.

I am not saying that the period when we are preparing to listen to God will have no effect on the way we pray.

John of the Cross, for instance, twice (Ascent of Mount Carmel 11.X111. Dark Night of the Soul 1.1X*)* tells us of the signs by which the soul is passing from meditation, ie the state when it is our own thoughts that are reflected in prayer, to contemplation, the state where God is directly speaking to us; and these include taking no pleasure in the work of the senses and developing a loving attentiveness upon God. In the same way the soul intent upon knowing God through charity may find itself no longer inclined to pray in the same way. Whereas before the ways of prayer seemed safe, if at times a little boring, it no longer feels the need to run through the routine which has previously served it well. It is possible, in fact, to come to a different definition of prayer altogether: prayer is whatever brings the soul closer to God, and for this no words may be necessary, he can be found through action alone. Extroversion, in other words, is saved. We can safely continue not to think of God as solely confined within prayer, but to be met also in the outside world.

This was certainly Thérèse's method. As a nun she would have been expected to take part in the normal prayerful activities of her order. But unlike her predecessors she left us with no special method of prayer by which we can come to know God. She certainly valued it highly, as we learn from her recollections confided to the mother of her order, describing it as a leap of the heart, a simple casting of the eyes towards heaven, words which show how spontaneous it was on her part, how far removed from anything we can learn in books. But it was not her main focus of attention, and this is why I say she is so important to the laity, who have to keep their senses open, who are required to serve God through charity and not solely through prayer.

This new definition of prayer, as whatever brings the soul closer to God - actually it is not so new. *The Tablet* recently quoted St Thomas Aquinas as saying, more than 700 years ago, that 'as long as one is acting in one's heart, speech or work in such a way as to tend towards God, one is praying'- this definition should not be taken as an excuse to abstain from prayer altogether, particularly in the early stages of the spiritual life, before one is fully committed, when other alternatives loom before one and seem more attractive than a life devoted to charity. And of course one can pray at any time, in answer to a heartfelt need, or wrestling with some difficult moral problem which one feels incapable of solving on one's own. In other words, there is no restriction on prayer, no time or situation when it cannot be practised. And one may arise with the problem solved, or with a solution in sight. But this does not necessarily mean that God has taken a hand in prayer, has directly intervened and presented one with the answer. It could be - indeed it is much more likely - that the mere fact of having laid the matter before him has given one the answer - in other words, it is one's own mind guiding one rather than any direct activity of God. This need for realism, for the absence of illusion, has been summed up by TS Eliot in *Ash Wednesday* when he has learnt - and it was a painful lesson on his part - that

> time is always time,
> and place is always and only place
> and what is actual is actual only for one time
> and only for one place,

In a similar way we have to reconcile ourselves to the fact that, at least in the early stages of the spiritual life, prayer is just that, an objective set of words that may or may not bring their reward, but that the inner reward, in all cases, is something that the individual mind devises. This will at least stop us feeling let down when our prayer seems to be going badly.

But where Aquinas' words can be of enormous benefit is in this in-between stage of the spiritual life, before we have developed the faculty of direct communication with God. For we may arise thoroughly dissatisfied with our moments of prayer, having failed to find adequate words, convinced that we were closer to God when we had a regular routine of prayer, and that we are now further from him than ever. It is then that we need to remind ourselves that as long as we are tending, at least in action, towards God, then this is our prayer, and that there is nothing wrong with the path of charity that we have chosen.

I earlier cited extroversion as the one essential prerequisite if we are to perfect ourselves through charity. But the word, like its opposite, introversion needs to be rid of the common connotations we give to it before it is fully understood. In ordinary parlance an extrovert (particularly, oddly enough, if one spells it this way rather than 'extravert', which is an alternative spelling) is a back-slapping individual, full of funny stories, who scarcely lets you get a word in and whose company you relish for his entertainment value before tastes suddenly turn and you wish he would go away. An introvert (here there is no alternative spelling) on the other hand is a quiet, possibly modest individual, who lets you talk and listens to what you say. He is an artist, possibly, a scholar, whom you are glad to welcome to your house. He can safely be left with the children, though you sometimes wish he was more outgoing, more ready to stimulate you.

These are the reputations the words have acquired, though their derivations are very much simpler. They both come from the Latin, one meaning turning outwards, the other turning inwards. Of the two, I have already suggested, we would prefer to be labelled introvert. There is something definitely pleasing about having one's own thoughts, a place to which we can safely retreat when we fancy it. There aren't many domains one can truly call one's own in this busy world, but this is one of them. But this is what one has to give up, however desirable it may seem, if one is to progress in the way of perfection.

Jesus makes precisely this point in Matthew 5:15, and the image is repeated in each of the three synoptic gospels, when he says

Nor do men light a lamp and put it under a bushel, but on a stand, and it gives light to all in the house. Let your light so shine before men, that they may see your good works and give glory to your father is in heaven.

And I have already cited the parable of the talents (Matt 25:14) where our inclination is to side with the third servant who hid his talent on the ground, where it would be perfectly safe from thieves; only to receive the severest punishments from his master.

This is certainly one of the hardest things for us to give up, this place where we feel perfectly safe with our own thoughts. Indeed we may not feel that we have to give it up at all: everybody has some refuge, don't they, we cannot be perpetually at every person's beck and call.

In some the quality of being introverted is something that arises naturally. They feel that there is nothing wrong with their behaviour, they are acting this way because they have always done so. In them, therefore, it may be a fault of the imagination rather than will, but the wake-up call is still as peremptory as it is to the others. They should come, once they have woken up to the demands of their religion, to realise that what seems natural to them, their sinking back into their old ways, was a type of selfishness. For there is nothing good in sinking back in this way. It is a form of evasion of responsibilities. There is too much work to be done in this world: we should at least try to play our part in it, however small it may be.

I have called it a wake up call. But another term which applies to it is conversion. Conversion, like sanctity, seems a word that we should apply to others. We automatically think of Paul, or Augustine, those who have gone through a grand conversion and left a record of it. But we forget that we ourselves undergo a conversion every time we go to the sacrament of reconciliation. There we confess our sins, confess, too, that we have left undone many of the things that we should have done, and pray to do better in the future.

So this is, in a way, a form of conversion; and included in the list of things we have left undone, if only we could bring ourselves to think of it, is the call to sanctity, the determination not simply to be a better Christian, but to aim at perfection. Sadly we do not realise this half the time. We think only of the things we have done, and welcome the relief which comes with the weight of them coming off our shoulders. And then we resume, more or less, the way of life to which we have become accustomed. But what we do not realise is that God's pardon brings with it another call, just as John the Baptist's did beside the river Jordan two thousand years ago. This is to embrace another way of life altogether, one in which we can no longer be satisfied with our mediocrities. Probably we should be rather scared if the thought were so much as to enter our mind, and should dismiss it as a thing for others to do. One less sin to worry about seems sufficient for us, one determination not to fall into the same sin again. What we fail to realise is that the process of a radical conversion applies to all Christians.

It is too important to be left in the hands of Paul, Augustine, and others of that magnitude. Yes, we may feel ourselves built on a lesser scale than they. We shall never, it seems, reach their heights, shall never, certainly, acquire the same title. But we have the same potentialities. And so I repeat, the Church of God is meant to be an assembly of people aiming after perfection, and not simply for the random and half-hearted, for those who ignore the call.

Lightning Source UK Ltd.
Milton Keynes UK
UKHW010629121120
373270UK00002B/348